Whimsical animals

DOLLS TO MAKE FROM FABRIC

By Miriam Gourley

C&T PUBLISHING

Copyright © 1993 Miriam Gourley

Edited by Harold Nadel
Technical information researched by Joyce Lytle
Photography by Leon Woodward, Photocraft, Orem, Utah
Illustrations by Mary Ellen Brown
Cover and book design by Rose Sheifer Graphic Productions, Walnut Creek, California

Ribbons furnished by Lion Ribbon and C. M. Offray & Son, Inc.
Fabric furnished by VIP Fabrics and Concord House Fabrics
Stuffing and batting furnished by Fairfield Processing, Inc.
Fabric paints furnished by Delta Technical Coatings, Inc.

This book is dedicated with love to my mother and father,
who felt that playtime was an essential ingredient for raising
well-balanced children.

Anchor embroidery floss is a registered trademark of J. P. Coats, Inc.
Bernina is a registered trademark of Fritz Gegauf, Ltd.
Cernit is a registered trademark of T and F GmbH.
Delta Ceramcoat, Cool Stuff, Fabric Dye, LiquidHearts, Starlite Dye, and Stencil Magic Paint
    Creme are registered trademarks of Delta Technical Coatings, Inc.
Fairfield Cotton Classic Batting and Polyfil Supreme are registered trademarks of Fairfield
    Processing, Inc.
Paper Clay is a registered trademark of Creative Paperclay Company.
Poly Pellets is a registered trademark of Fairfield Processing, Inc.
Sculpey is a registered trademark of Polyform Products.
Sulky Iron-On Transfer Pen is a registered trademark of Sulky of America.
Velcro is a registered trademark of Velcro USA Inc.

ISBN 0-914881-61-2

Library of Congress Catalog Card Number: 92-42062
Library of Congress Cataloging-in-Publication Data

Gourley, Miriam, 1951-
        Whimsical animals : dolls to make from fabric / by Miriam Gourley.
            p.   cm.
        ISBN 0-914881-61-2 : $15.95
            1. Soft toy making.   2. Stuffed animals (Toys)   I. Title.
TT174.3.G68   1993
745.592 ' 4—dc20   92-42062
                                                                          CIP

Published by C & T Publishing
P. O. Box 1456
Lafayette, California 94549

Printed in The United States of America
10 9 8 7 6 5 4 3 2 1

TABLE OF CONTENTS

•

	TEXT	PATTERNS

INTRODUCTION

animal stories have delighted many generations of children and adults. Most of us have grown up with *Peter Rabbit, The Wind in the Willows, Lightfoot the Deer,* Roald Dahl's *Mr. Fox,* and other books that portray animals as having human traits. Children and adults still enjoy creating and playing with animals dressed in clothing and living in charming little forest cottages. This book contains patterns and instructions to help you create your own animals, furniture, and cottages. There are two main kinds of animals: most are all-cloth, while some have Paper Clay® or polymer heads. You will also learn about new stuffing materials, textured paints, and unique embellishments.

The first seventeen years of my life were spent on a ranch in southern Colorado. I was the eldest of eight children and experienced an idyllic childhood. Although my parents preferred the quiet farm life, they had traveled quite a bit and experienced many cultures. My father was interested in carpentry and had a shop full of woodworking equipment. My mother had a degree in art and English, so we were exposed to good literature and hands-on art from the time we were small. Both of my parents encouraged our vivid imaginations. I remember my mother telling us the snow-covered trees looked like a fairyland: since the Colorado winters sometimes reached 30° below zero, that was a very positive view of winter. I always preferred outdoor chores to household duties, and I spent many hours helping my father tend the farm animals and the fields.

Early in my life, I discovered that animals have distinct personalities. Cows were my favorites, because they were usually so co-operative. Of course, that may have been because they were in a hurry to get to the barn to be milked or to leave for the pasture in the morning. Sheep, on the other hand, seemed to use any means to frustrate their shepherds; just when you were a few yards from the wide-open gate, one of these seemingly docile animals would find a hole in the fence and lead all his friends through it. We were elated when our father decided to quit raising sheep. (You will notice that a sheep doll is conspicuously absent from the patterns included in this book.) Our farm, however, had no shortages of mice, rabbits, and other non-domesticated animals; once, I encountered a badger while I was driving a tractor out in the field. We also owned a few pigs, a dog, a barn full of cats, and some chickens. When I was quite young, I took two baby chicks from their nest so my sister Sonia and I could hold them. I was immediately attacked by an unhappy mother hen who proceeded to knock me down, beat me with her wings, and peck at me. This led to a life-long phobia of chickens and other feathered friends, so I'm sure you wonder why I have included the pheasant and the nightingale in the book; I can only suppose that it's because I still like birds better than sheep.

When I began planning the animals for this book, I decided to name my creations after some of my favorite relatives and friends. My immediate family and a large extended family, as well as many friends, furnish unlimited inspiration. Each of my animals will be introduced with a story, and I hope you will use these patterns to recreate moments and people from your own history.

You will make friends with Florence, a cranky but well-meaning nightingale who nurtures Butch the Warthog back to health with homemade soup. (She also nags him about his housekeeping habits.) No animal book would be complete without cats: you will meet a variety of cats, not all domesticated. I created four flamboyant barn cats and a rather exotic-looking lion named Mephisto. The barn cat pattern was interpreted by several wonderful designers. In addition, you will meet a giraffe named Uncle Wayne, a lively coyote who plans all the neighborhood parties, a mathematician pig, two Victorian mice, a tamed chicken, a fox, a hound dog, and several other amazing creatures.

People who find satisfaction in creating dolls and animals also seem to enjoy collecting materials—not just fabrics, but beads, sequins, antique lace, old jewelry, ribbons, paints, clay, feathers, shells, and much more. Barbara Johnston boiled a goose carcass, then buried the skeleton in an ant hill to finish cleaning the bones. She unearthed the remains and kept the neck bones in little drawers until the right doll-making project came along. Sure enough, her friend Tracy Stilwell used one of the bones to create a head for a 5" doll which was christened Bone Head. My personal hoard doesn't include goose neck bones, but I have brass wire eyeglasses, little boxes of teddy bear eyes, ceramic buttons, cabinets of embroidery floss, wool fiber in a myriad of exotic colors, piles of fabrics, metallic threads, colorful yarns, and many other items tucked away throughout my house.

During the past few years, interest has grown in sculpting dolls and animals from various kinds of polymer clays. Many doll makers have begun to experiment with these clays, which can be cured in regular kitchen ovens rather than kilns. Some of these products, such as Sculpey® and Cernit®, are increasing in popularity. I recently discovered a wonderful new product called Paper Clay. My family noticed how much fun I was having with this product and dropped all kinds of hints; finally, I agreed to let them participate. All four of my children made animal heads. When some my children's friends saw our creations, they also wanted to "help"; my husband, Bruce, decided it wasn't fair to let the kids play with all this good stuff alone, so he sat down to play with them. Among the animals created by this gifted group are Felix Romero del Gato, by my ten-year-old son Clinton. Butch the Warthog was created by Thomas, our thirteen-year-old who wanted to create an Australian animal. Vanessa, who is eight, made Ellie Elephant, complete with pink, sparkly ears. Michael, the five-year-old, tried making an elephant, which somehow turned into a snowman. His second attempt at animal design was somewhat more rewarding, and he created a very charming mouse. I designed Arthur, a mathematician named for my late Uncle Arthur who collected minerals and fossils. My husband is an old hand at sculpting, but he hadn't tried anything like this before. After perusing *National Geographic* and several children's story books, he sculpted the heads, let them dry, and painted them (his first painting attempt). I think the results are very impressive. The Jensen children spent several hours molding and painting their animal heads: Kyle made the turtle; Ben created Henny Penny and helped his youngest sister Mindy make the fox. Jill Jensen made a little dog and we decorated her with pink ribbon. In fact, while the young Jensens were working on the animals, one more little neighborhood friend wanted to contribute. Brent Staley made the brown dinosaur, which I dressed in hand-painted fabric and hand-spun yarns. In addition, I asked artists Betts Vidal and Kim Brown to create animals using one of the polymer clays. Their wonderful results are pictured on pages 35 and 46.

After the animal heads were finished, I sewed bodies for them and made simple clothing. In Chapter 3, you will see several basic body and clothing patterns for Paper Clay animals. I have also included a few diagrams as a guideline for heads.

Part of my childhood play included designing living spaces. Sometimes they were for little plastic animals, sometimes for dolls, and sometimes just for enjoyment. My mother allowed us to cut up the outdated Sears catalogues and we pasted pictures of drapes and other furnishings into shoe boxes. Sometimes we glued cardboard partitions to make two rooms. A peep hole was cut in one end and a window in the box lid. We glued colored cellophane over the window and it gave the room a wonderful glow. We made a big mess, but this kind of play entertained us for hours.

The furniture and cottages for this book were created by my husband. You will learn how to transform an oatmeal box into a tiny forest cottage, and how to create wonderful furniture from willow and other items which you can purchase at a florist shop or find on a roadside. Complete instructions are included, along with color photographs and numerous illustrations.

The animal patterns, information on techniques and materials, drawings and photographs should be enough fodder for many hours of creative play, so gather your fabric, equipment, and hoard of trinkets, and get busy!

•

CHAPTER ONE

LARGE CLOTH ANIMALS

Note: All the animals are sewn with a ¼" seam allowance unless otherwise stated.

A Word about Fabric Choice

There are no rules regarding appropriate fabrics for creating the animals in this book. Choose fabrics which intrigue you and which seem right for the specific animal. The scale of the fabric is a consideration: as a general rule, use smaller prints for smaller animals. Don't worry too much about whether the fabrics match your decor exactly. Choosing fabrics can be a wonderful part of your playtime. Many quilt shops and fabric stores sell fat quarters (quarter-yard cuts that are approximately 22" x 18"), which is a fairly inexpensive way to buy several kinds of fabrics large enough to play with. Lay them together in groups. Experiment freely by adding solids and prints and deleting weak choices. Add ribbons, paint swatches, and trims to the overall picture. Experience is a very good teacher, but I have also learned about color theories by talking to other artists and reading their books. When I was at the Vermont Quilt Festival, I had a chance to spend some time with quilt artist Roberta Horton. When she wants to enhance a beautiful floral, she combines it with plaids and/or stripes. I suppose I had been doing that accidentally or perhaps instinctively, but she made me more aware of the effect of one pattern upon another.

The only caution I would give about fabric choice concerns texture; if you are making a small body, don't select a stiff, thick fabric, because it will be difficult to turn right side out. Cottons or silks are available in a wide range of wonderful colors and patterns, and will be easy to work with. They can easily be combined with other textures and fibers for interesting and beautiful results.

Alternative Stuffing Materials

As children, many of us played with beanbags. For some, it was a sewing exercise; for others, it was an game to be played indoors during rainy weather. I always liked feeling the beans as they shifted in the bag when I tilted it back and forth in my hands. For several years, designer Becky Tuttle has been creating a series of animal dolls called "On a Roll" because of their rounded lower bodies. The bodies are weighted with scented rice or plastic pellets to give them stability. Dolls containing rice, beans, birdseed, or plastic pellets can be posed easily. I have used Poly Pellets® to stuff the cats in this book and give them a very laid-back personality. Here are some tips for using any of the above-mentioned products as an alternative to, or in addition to, regular stuffing:

1. Do not fill the arm, leg, or tail to the top. In order to have the maximum effect, the body part should not be over two-thirds full.
2. Stuffing may be used in conjunction with the pellets, rice, or beans.
3. Do not use pellets or similar products to stuff items which will be given to small children, since they may chew the animal open and spill the filling into their mouths.
4. Create a funnel from stiff paper or use a plastic kitchen funnel to fill the animal's body cavity with the pellets or other products.

BARN CATS

Cats were a big part of my youth; we always stumbled over a big group of them as we went out the back door. My mother taught us a funny song called *Don Gato,* which told the story of a romantic cat who read his love letters atop a high red roof. One particular day, he was reading a letter from his lady cat who had just accepted his proposal of marriage. Don was so elated, he jumped up and consequently fell off the roof. The doctor cats all attended him, but in vain; Don Gato died but, as the funeral passed the market square, the smell of fish brought him back to life.

My favorite cats, however, were what we called our "barn cats." These cats were born and lived most of their lives in the barn where we milked the cows. They were a rather wild lot and didn't socialize with humans. They did accept our offerings of milk, but the rest of their diet consisted of mice. I always rather liked their independent nature and decided they would make good characters for this book.

Barbara Johnston, publisher and editor of *Dollmaker's Journal,* created two teenage cats from Texas who are making their first visit to a mall in southern California. Barbara writes, "Kitty Blue and Dotty are two teenagers from Mewlshoe, Texas. They have come to California to visit their Aunt Tabby (Miss Texas Tornado of 1954). The cousins are on the way to the mall to check out the action and have dressed the way they feel true California teens would be costumed.

"Kitty Blue wears a brand-new hand-knit sweater with a matching hat—a gift from Aunt Tabby—and has added her own touch of veiling. Aunt Tabby did Kitty's nails this morning at the breakfast table, after cleaning up a plate of pickled herring. Kitty Blue sports a cowboy boot pin so she won't get homesick for Mewlshoe.

"Dotty has overdone her dime-store make-up just a tad, using the techniques she learned in the preliminaries of the *Miss Teen Catnip Patch* pageant this spring. Dotty is a firm believer in the theory that 'if a little is good, more is surely better,' especially when it comes to decoration. Lavender eye shadow is her particular favorite, since it coordinates with her leggings. Her best girlfriend, Mewlissa, gave her a new perm before the trip. Dotty never goes anywhere without her pet armadillo, Spot, and bought him a new blue sequin collar for this memorable trip." You will notice Barbara's clever use of false eyelashes, trimmed to fit the cats' eyes, as well as false fingernails and glitzy yarns.

Patti Culia's cat is called "What Bird!?" and still has feathers clutched in her paw and hanging out of the corner of her mouth. My son Thomas said he thought he'd seen her on a billboard in Las Vegas. My friend Paula said she thought the cat might be the lead in the Broadway musical *Cats.* Patti's use of color is stunning. She took a silk-dyeing class

and decided to try the dyes on muslin. She blotted the brushes on a piece of silk and was so enchanted with the results that she embellished the silk with beads and Brazilian embroidery to create a beautiful vest.

Morgan, Bonnie Hoover's cat, is dressed in black and white with an accent color—Bonnie's favorite color combination. Bonnie's forte is embellishment, and this cat's face and clothing are accented with wonderful and unusual items. The cheeks are fabric which is fused to the face, the mouth is embroidered, and Bonnie added whiskers.

Tracy Stilwell's dolls always have an aura of mystery and magic. Tracy's magical cat, Polly, has a body of hand-painted fabric and her clothing is VIP's Halloween fabric. Polly is accompanied by her little "spirit guide" and she carries a bag full of magic. Her eyes and mouth are appliquéd to her face, and her pupils are sequins and beads.

Karen Wooton's slinky feline is called Cathouse Sunday. Karen loved the marbled fabrics and thought they added interest to the cat. When the body was finished, they went shopping for clothing; the cat wanted something that wouldn't hide her beautiful body, so she selected the very sheer chiffon. She also demanded the feathers and sequined undergarments. Karen's son observed that she looked like a working girl. He didn't choose quite that term, but Karen felt the cat was a seasoned veteran at catting around. Karen said, "I realize that with her profession and all, she may not fit in with some of the other ladies and gentlemen that will be visiting you, but she does have a heart of gold."

The various interpretations of this barn cat pattern should give you many ideas. Don't restrict these ideas to the cats: have fun with all the other animals, too.

Materials Requirements

◆ ⅓ yard of fabric for each body
◆ Approximately 1½ cups of plastic pellets, bird-seed, rice, or beans
◆ Fairfield Polyfil Supreme® or other stuffing
◆ Quilting thread
◆ 2" needle for sculpting
◆ Delta® fabric paints (see the painting chart for exact colors used)
◆ Black Sulky Iron-On Transfer Pen®
◆ Tracing paper

Assembly Instructions

1. Use the transfer pen to trace the torso shape onto a piece of paper. Include the cat's face and the dots (which indicate the arm openings). If you are making the lion, use the pen to outline the head and features. Set the iron to a moderately hot setting, depending on the fabric you have chosen. (I used the cotton setting.) After the ink dries, place the paper with the ink side down on the right side of the fabric. Place the iron on the paper and move it slowly from one area to the next to avoid scorching. Carefully lift up a corner of the paper from time to time to see if the outline is dark enough.

2. Cut out the torso and pin it right side down on the right side of a rectangular piece of fabric (10½" x 6") for the torso back. Stitch around the torso, leaving the bottom and arm holes open as illustrated.

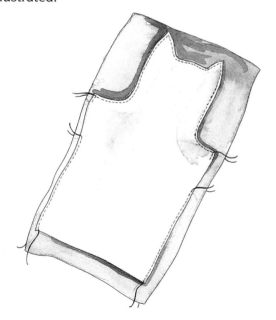

Trim the seam allowance to ⅛" and clip the corners. Do not turn the torso right side out. Set it aside.

3. Place the arms with right sides together and stitch around them, leaving the top open to turn. Trim the seam allowance to ⅛" and clip between the round areas of the paws. Turn the arms right side out.

4. Insert the stuffing into the round areas of the paw so there is about ½" of stuffing at the bottom.

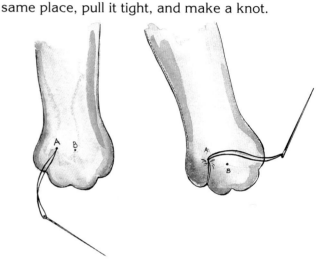

   Thread a needle with quilting thread and double it. Make a knot at the end. Bring the needle up between the curves of the paws at point A, about ½" from the center point between the curves. Wrap the thread around the end of the paw, bring the needle up through the same place, pull it tight, and make a knot.

   Do not cut the thread; insert the needle close to where you made the knot and bring it out at point B.

   Re-insert the needle, catch two or three threads to anchor it, and bring the thread around the end of the paw as you did previously. Repeat this procedure until all three areas have been sculpted.

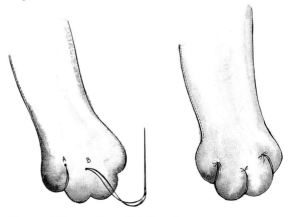

Repeat Steps 3 and 4 for the legs.

5. Measure three tablespoons of the pellets and pour them into the arm. The arm should be about two-thirds full. Add more pellets if necessary. See page 6 for more information on using pellets. Stitch across the top of the arm so the pellets will not fall out. Repeat this procedure for the legs, but use ½ cup of pellets for each leg.

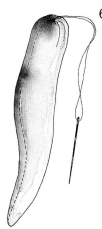

6. Place the tail pieces with right sides together and stitch around them, leaving an opening at the top. Trim the seam allowance to ⅛" and turn the tail right side out. Fill the tail with ¼ cup of pellets, fold ¼" of the opening inward, and hand gather the tail. Pull the gathers tight and tie a knot. Set the tail aside.

7. Insert one arm at a time into the torso and pin it in place. Stitch the arm into the armhole as shown.

8. Pin the legs to the front bottom edge of the torso so they are curved toward each other as shown.

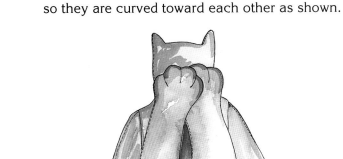

Machine stitch the legs to the torso and stuff the cat's head and torso (with regular stuffing) to within 1" of the opening. Measure ¼ cup of pellets and carefully pour them into the lower torso. Fold under ¼" of the lower back side of the torso and pin it to the leg seam, covering the previous stitching. Hand stitch the torso closed.

9. After the knickers or pantaloons are on the cat, stitch the tail to the cat's back (through the clothing and into the body) about 1½" above the center of the lower edge of the torso.

10. Paint the cat's face using the following diagram as a guide line. (Feel free to use your own color scheme and face design.)

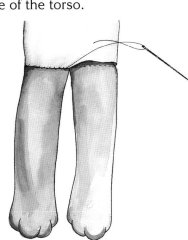

Part of Body	Copper Lady Cat	Blue Boy Cat
Iris	Starlite Dye™ Violet	Fabric Dye® English Yew
Eyelid	Starlite Dye Gold	Same
Pupils, dots by mouth, mouth, and eye outline	Fabric Dye Black	Same
Whites of eyes, dot by eyes, and highlight in pupil	Fabric Dye White	Same
Right half of Lady Cat face	Fabric Dye Black	
Left half of Lady Cat face	Starlite Dye Brown	

The calico effect was achieved by randomly using black Delta Fabric Dye and brown Delta Starlite Dye. I used a medium-size brush to stipple the colors.

Stripes		Starlite Dye Brown
Nose	Fabric Dye Adobe	Same
Inside of ears	unpainted	Fabric Dyes Light Brown and White

The pink cat is called Christine, named after one of my favorite cousins. She loves beautiful clothes and the color purple. (It is not surprising that her boyfriend Stan is a purple cat.) Christine and Stan are painted in much the same way as the other two cats, with the following changes:

Part of Body	Christine	Stan
Iris	Starlite Dye Brown	Starlite Dye Kelly
Right side of Christine's face	Fabric Dye Light Mauve	
Left side of Christine's face	Fabric Dye Black	
Stan's stripes		Starlite Dye Violet
Inside of ears	unpainted	Starlite Dye Violet and Fabric Dye White

The iris and other small areas may be painted by using a very fine brush, such as a size 000.

CLOTHING

Materials Requirements

KNICKERS AND PANTALOONS
✦ ¼ yard of fabric
✦ ⅓ yard of 1¼"-wide eyelet lace for pantaloons
✦ ⅓ yard of ¼"-wide satin ribbon for pantaloons
✦ 2 ribbon roses (⅜"-wide) for pantaloons
✦ 9½" of ¼"-wide elastic

SAILOR SHIRT OR DRESS
✦ ⅓ yard of fabric for the shirt
✦ ½ yard of fabric for the dress
✦ ½ yard of 1"-wide ribbon (satin or grosgrain)
✦ 1 yard of ¼"-wide satin ribbon for the shirt
✦ ⅔ yard of ¼"-wide satin ribbon for the dress
✦ Velcro® or snaps for back closure
✦ Small buttons to decorate the back edge (optional)

Assembly Instructions

KNICKERS

1. Gather the lower edge of each leg to fit the leg band. Press under one edge of each leg band ¼". Place the leg band and the gathered knickers leg with right sides together, matching the raw edges, and stitch them together.

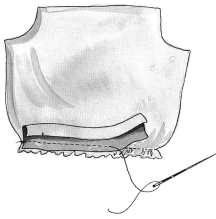

2. Place the knickers right sides together and stitch the front and back center seams. Clip the curves and press the seams open.

3a. Place the knickers right sides together and stitch the inseam.

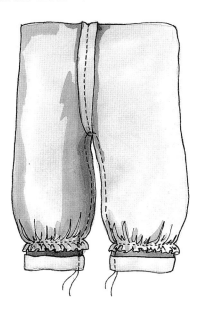

3b. Fold the pressed edge of the cuffs over the raw gathered edges of the knickers and hand stitch the band in place.

4. Zigzag the top edge of the knickers to finish the raw edges. Fold the top edge toward the inside of the knickers to form a ½"-wide casing. Stitch close to the zigzagged edge, leaving a 1" opening so you can insert the elastic. Use a small brass safety pin or bodkin to thread the elastic through the casing. Overlap the ends of the elastic about ½" and stitch them together by hand, using strong quilting thread. Finish stitching the casing and place the knickers on the cat.

PANTALOONS

1. Cut two 5⅜" pieces of eyelet lace for the leg bands. Follow the instructions for the knickers, Steps 1, 2, 3a, and 4.
2. Use the ¼"-wide satin ribbon to tie two bows approximately 1½"-wide. Trim the ends at 45° angles. Glue each bow to the front of the pantaloon at the top of the lace. Glue a small ribbon rose at the center of the bow.

SAILOR SHIRT

1. Apply the ¼"-wide satin ribbon to the cuffs, hip band, and collar, as indicated on the pattern pieces. Check your machine to see if you have a special presser foot to make the stitching easier. (Foot #5 is a great help for Bernina® users.) You will need to make a slight tuck in the ribbon on the collar where the angle changes. (It is easier to press the cuffs and hip band in half before you stitch the ribbon, since the crease helps with ribbon placement.)

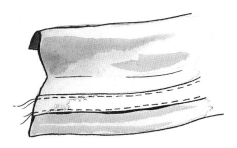

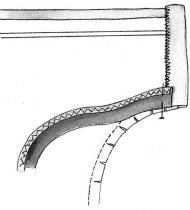

2. Place the collar and collar lining pieces with right sides together and stitch around them, leaving the neck opening unstitched. Trim the seam allowance to ⅛" and turn it right side out. Press the collar and set it aside. Repeat for the other half of the collar.

3. Stitch the shoulder seams of the yoke and press them open. Zigzag the back edges of the yoke (which will be used as a facing). Place the collar pieces on the yoke, with the front edges together, and baste them in place.

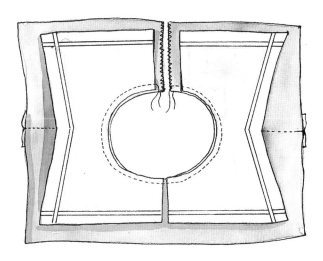

4. Cut a bias strip 1¼" x 12" and press under ¼" Zigzag the pressed edge. Fold the back center edge of the yoke back so there is ¼" between the back edge of the collar and the folded edge of the yoke.

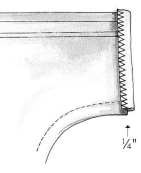

Clip the curves of the neck edge and, with right sides together, pin the raw edge of the bias strip to the neck edge, overlapping the zigzagged yoke back edge. Stitch the bias strip to the neck edge through all thicknesses.

Trim the seam allowance and turn the bias strip to the wrong side of the shirt to form a facing. Fold the back center edge toward the wrong side of the shirt to form a facing. Lift the collar and top stitch the shirt to the facing, close to the neck seam.

5. Gather the top edge of the shirt front to fit the yoke front. Place the shirt front and yoke with right sides together and stitch them. Repeat for the shirt back pieces. Trim the seam allowance to ⅛" and press it toward the yoke.

6. Gather the bottom edges of the sleeves to fit the cuffs. Press under ¼" of the cuff edge furthest from the ribbon. Place the gathered edge of the sleeve and the ribbon side of the cuff with right sides together and stitch them. Press the seam allowance toward the cuff.

7. Gather the top edges of the sleeves to fit the sleeve opening. Place the sleeve and shirt with right sides together and stitch them. Trim the seam allowance and press it toward the yoke.

8. Fold the shirt with right sides together and stitch from the cuffs to the lower edge of the shirt. Press the seams open and fold the pressed edge of the cuff over the raw edges of the sleeve. Stitch the cuff in place.

9. Gather the lower edge of the shirt to fit the hip band. Press under the lower edge of the hip band (the side furthest from the ribbon) and stitch it to the lower shirt edge as you did for the cuffs. Fold the hip band in half with right sides together and stitch the ends with a ½" seam allowance.

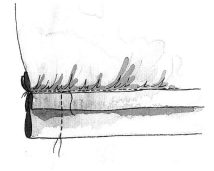

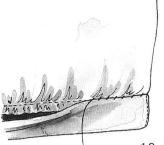

Clip the corners of the hip band and zigzag the back center edges of the shirt. Turn the band right side out and stitch the folded edge over the raw edges of the gathers.

10. Press the back edge of the shirt and lap the left side over the right, making sure the back edges of the collar are touching. Stitch snaps or Velcro to close the back edge. If you wish, you may purchase small buttons to finish the back. Cut two 7¾" ties from the 1" ribbon. Fold under ¼" and stitch the ribbon to the shoulder seam under the collar, next to the neck edge. Make a square knot about 2" from the ends of the ties and clip the ends at a 45° angle.

DRESS

Follow the directions for the Sailor Shirt, Steps 1-8 and 10. Zigzag the lower edge of the dress and press up a ⅝" hem. Blind stitch the hem by hand or machine. If you want to add eyelet lace, stitch it to the lower edge of the dress and make a ½" tuck by folding 1" of the lower edge of the dress toward the inside and stitching ½" from the folded edge. Press the tuck toward the lace.

MEPHISTO

Mephisto is an appropriate name for this mysterious and intimidating king of the jungle. His roar is known and feared by many of the neighborhood children—and a few adults; but underneath the ferocious temper lies a generous and sensitive heart. The woven Zulu love beads which Mephisto wears on his vest are a means of communication. Each colored bead contains a distinct message: red means intense love ("My heart bleeds for you"), green indicates "I have become as thin as a blade of grass, from pining for you," and black communicates anger, hurt, or jealousy. Mephisto's love letter was a gift from a Zulu princess he met during a tour of Africa. (He must have made quite an impression!) His one true love is a pretty blonde lioness who swoons when he serenades her with romantic Italian arias.

Materials Requirements

- ✦ ⅓ yard of fabric for the body
- ✦ ¼ yard of fabric for the knickers
- ✦ 9½" of ¼"-wide elastic
- ✦ Scrap of fabric for the vest and sleeves
- ✦ Approximately 1½ cups of plastic pellets, birdseed, rice, or beans
- ✦ Stuffing
- ✦ Quilting thread
- ✦ Delta fabric paints (See the painting chart for the exact colors used.)
- ✦ Sulky Iron-On Transfer Pen
- ✦ Brown fine-tip permanent-ink felt pen
- ✦ Textured yarn for the mane and tail
- ✦ Tracing paper

Assembly Instructions

1. Follow the instructions for the Barn Cats on page 8, Step 1. You will have cut three of the head shapes, including the face. Pin the face onto one of the other head shapes, with the right side facing you. Use black thread and top stitch the outline of the nose and upper mouth.

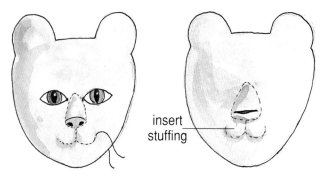

insert
stuffing

Make a slit on the back of the nose and stuff it firmly, using a small stuffing tool such as a bamboo skewer. Sew the slit shut as illustrated.

Insert stuffing between the face and second layer, and push it into the upper lip area on each side of the face.

Place the face and back of head with right sides together and stitch around the head, leaving an opening as indicated on the pattern piece. Trim the seam allowance, clip the angles, and turn the face right side out. Stuff the ears lightly and top stitch them as indicated on the pattern piece. Continue stuffing the head until it is firm, then sew the opening closed.

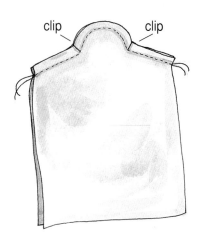

clip   clip

2. With right sides together, pin the torso pieces together and stitch the shoulder seams.

Follow the instructions for the Barn Cats, Steps 3-5.

3. Insert one arm at a time into the torso and pin it in place. Stitch the side seams of the torso as illustrated.

4. Stitch the legs to the body, following the instructions for the Barn Cats, Step 8.

5. Pin the head to the neck. With strong, matching quilting thread, stitch the head in place. Starting at the back of the head, stitch the head to the neck tab; work your way around the head, under the chin, and then around to the back of the head. If the head is wobbly, repeat the procedure, ⅛" from the first line of stitches.

6. Cut a piece of fabric 5½" x 1½" for the tail. Press both short ends under ¼" and fold the fabric in half lengthwise, right sides together. Stitch along the sides, trim the seam allowance, and turn the tail right side out. Cut several 6" lengths of yarn, tie a piece around the center, and fold the yarn in half. Stitch the yarn to the tail as illustrated.

7. After the lion has his clothing, stitch the other end of the tail to the lion about 1" below the knickers casing, on the back center seam.

Body Part	Paint Color
Whites of eyes and pupil highlight	Fabric Dye White
Iris	Starlite Dye Gold
Pupil, outline of outer eye, and nostrils	Fabric Dye Black
Dots on upper lip	Brown fine-tip permanent-ink felt pen
Lower nose and inside of ears	Fabric Dye White mixed with Starlite Dye Brown (equal amounts)

8. Paint the lion's face using the following diagram as a guideline:

peach

gold

white

black

peach

brown

9. Wind yarn around your four fingers (or a 4"-wide card) four times and tie a knot in the middle. If the yarn is narrow, you may want to wind it several more times. Attach these bundles of yarn around Mephisto's face for a handsome mane.

Clothing

Follow the directions for the knickers on page 11.

SLEEVED VEST

1. Place the vest pieces with right sides together and stitch the shoulder and side seams. Repeat for the vest lining. Press the seams open.
2. Place the vest and the lining with right sides together and stitch around the outside edges. Clip the curves. Turn the vest right side out and press it.

3. Place the sleeves with right sides together and stitch the underarm seam.

Press the underarm seam open and fold up ¼" of the lower edge of the sleeve. Fold up ¼" again and hand or machine stitch the hem. Gather the top edge of the sleeve and place it inside the vest, with right sides together. Baste the sleeve in place, if necessary, then machine stitch it. Trim the seam allowance and turn the vest right side out. Place the vest on Mephisto, leaving it open in front. If you don't happen to have a spare Zulu love letter, use an old brooch or make your own from a collage of antique buttons.

L. THORWALD FROGG

L. Thorwald Frogg, called Thor by his friends, is a dignified frog who works as a chemical engineer in a laboratory in the mountains of New Mexico. He spends his spare time trout fishing and writing humorous memoirs of his former life in a Texas swamp. Thorwald was also the middle name of his father, paternal grandfather, and great-grandfather. Much of his genealogy is traced back to Denmark but, since Frogg is not a Danish surname, we suspect there are other nationalities in his lineage—perhaps even Welsh. Thor enjoys living in the West where his legs are relatively safe from becoming someone's dinner.

Materials Requirements

♦ ⅓ yard of fabric for the body
♦ ¼ yard of fabric for the trousers
♦ Scrap of fabric to line the upper trousers
♦ Scrap of fabric for the collar
♦ Two ½" buttons
♦ ¼ yard of ¼"-wide satin ribbon
♦ ¼ yard of 1½"-wide satin ribbon for bow tie
♦ Anchor® embroidery floss in the following colors: #0907 gold, 0263 olive green, 02 white, and 403 black
♦ Delta Starlite Dye Violet
♦ Stuffing
♦ Small amount of plastic pellets
♦ Black Sulky Iron-On Transfer Pen
♦ Tracing paper

Assembly Instructions

1. Place the arms with right sides together and stitch around the entire piece, leaving an opening at the top for turning. Trim, clip the curves, and turn the arm right side out.

2. Top stitch the webbed area of the hands, and stuff the finger areas by adding very small amounts of stuffing at a time and packing it firmly. Stuff the arms to 1" above the top stitched area.

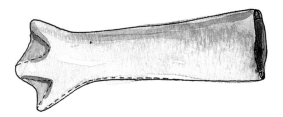

3. Fill the arm two-thirds to the top with plastic pellets. This will take 1 to 2 tablespoons per arm. Baste across the top of the arms to keep the pellets from falling out. Set the arms aside.

4. Assemble the legs in the same way, except you will fill the legs with stuffing to within 1" of the top of the leg. (I didn't use pellets in the legs.) Baste across the tops of the legs and set them aside.

5. Use the Sulky Iron-On Transfer Pen or other method to transfer the face and body outline to the fabric. Some people prefer to embroider the face before they sew it. Use a single strand of each color of thread and embroider as follows:

Body Part	Color	Stitch Type
Iris	Gold	Satin
Pupil	Black	Satin
Mouth	Olive Green	Back stitch
Pupil highlight	White	Two single stitches

Cut the body out and place the pieces with right sides together. Stitch the shoulder and head seams.

6. Place the arms inside the body so that the upper edge of the arms and the shoulder seams touch. Pin them in place. Stitch the side seams of the body.

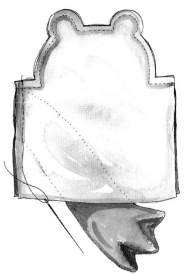

7. Assemble the upper trousers by placing them right sides together and stitching the side seams. Press the seams open and repeat the procedure for the trouser linings.

8. Place the upper trousers and lining with right sides together, matching the side seams, and stitch the upper edge.

9. Trim the seam allowance, clip the angles, and turn the upper trousers right side out. Press them and place the upper trousers over the frog's lower body, matching the raw edges. Baste the raw edges together. Fold the lining down in the front so the two points are facing the bottom edge of the frog. Stitch the buttons onto the trousers, through the upper trousers and front body of the frog. Or the points can face up, as shown on page 15.

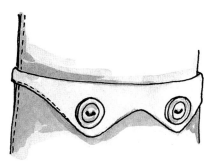

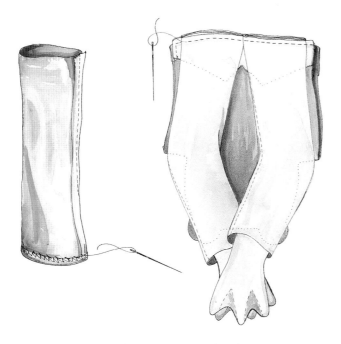

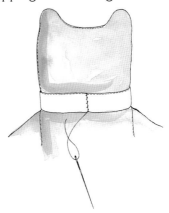

Trim the seam allowance, clip the angles, and turn the collar right side out. Press it and wrap it around the frog's neck with the finished end overlapping the raw edge in the back.

10. Cut two 9" x 5½" rectangles for the trouser legs. Zigzag the short edge and fold the rectangle lengthwise with right sides together. Stitch the back seam and fold up ¼" of the zigzagged edge. Blind stitch the lower edge and turn the leg right side out. Press the trouser leg and put it on the frog's leg, with the seam toward the back. The frog's leg should be centered inside the trouser leg. Baste through all layers and pin the legs to the front side of the unstuffed frog body.

Hand stitch the collar in place and tack it to the frog's body. Pull the collar down in the front so the points don't cover his mouth. Tack the collar in place in the front.

13. Wrap the ¼"-wide satin ribbon around the collar, centering it. Overlap the ends of the ribbon in front and glue it in place.

14. Make a 2¾"-wide satin bow from 1½"-wide satin ribbon, using the directions for the bow tie for Uncle Wayne on page 22. Glue the bow tie to the center front of the collar.

15. Paint the frog's eyelids purple. He's now ready to go fly fishing!

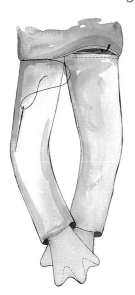

11. Machine stitch the legs to the front of the body and stuff the body firmly. Use small amounts of stuffing to stuff the eyes first, then the rest of the body. Fold under the raw edges of the back of the frog's body and pin the folded edge to the back of the frog's bottom seam, covering the stitching. Stitch the opening closed.

JEANNIE — FOREVER A SPRING CHICK

This beautiful chick, Jeannie, is a former model who took her Colorado farming community by storm. She was tall, graceful, well-dressed, and always a topic of conversation. Some of the older hens in the community thought her dresses were too short and her lipstick too bright. All the younger chicks idolized her and wanted to look just like her when they grew up. All the young males wished to date someone like Jeannie. As you can see by the picture on page 48, Paul is howling his approval and Uncle Wayne is quietly admiring how she saunters down the street.

12. Place the collar pieces with right sides together and stitch around, leaving an opening on one end.

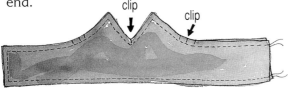

Materials Requirements

✦ ⅓ yard of fabric for the body and wings
✦ 10" x 12" piece of fabric for the legs
✦ Scrap of red fabric for the comb

- ✦ ⅓ yard for the dress
- ✦ Button for the brooch
- ✦ 22" of 4"-wide antique lace for the shawl
- ✦ ⅔ yard of 1½"-wide ribbon for ruffle
- ✦ Stuffing
- ✦ Delta fabric paint (see the paint chart)
- ✦ Small paint brushes (size 000 and ⅜")

Assembly Instructions

1. Place the body with right sides together and stitch it, leaving both legs open, as well as a side opening for turning. Trim the seam allowance and clip the curves. Set the body aside without turning it right side out.
2. Place the legs with right sides together and stitch them. Trim the seam allowance and clip the curves. Turn the legs right side out and stuff them firmly within ¾" of the top. Insert the legs, one at a time, through the side opening of the body and into the leg opening. Stitch across the legs.

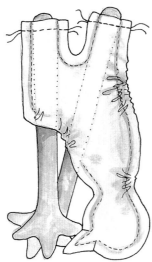

Turn the body right side out and stuff it firmly. Sew the side opening shut.

3. Paint the head in the following manner:

Part of Body	Paint Color
Beak	Ceramcoat® Yellow
Eyelid	Starlite Dye Brown
Pupil	Fabric Dye Black
Highlight in pupil	Fabric Dye White
Iris	Fabric Dye English Yew

4. Place the arms with the right side together and stitch them, leaving a side opening for turning. Trim the seam allowance and turn the arms right side out. Top stitch the fingers, which are indicated on the pattern piece. Insert small amounts of stuffing and fill the finger areas, then stuff the rest of the arm lightly. Stitch the opening closed and stitch the arms to the shoulders so they are floppy.
5. Place the comb with right sides together and stitch, leaving a small opening at the bottom. Trim the seam allowance, clip the curves, and turn the comb right side out. Stuff it and stitch the opening closed. Stitch or glue the comb to the top of the chicken's head.

Clothing

1. Place the dress pieces with right sides together and stitch the shoulder seams. Zigzag the neck opening and the sleeve openings to finish the raw edges. Stitch the side seams and fold the neck edge inward ¼". Fold under ¼" of the sleeves and hem them by machine or by hand.
2. Gather the top edge of the ribbon to fit the bottom hem line of the dress. Place the gathered ribbon and the dress with right sides together and zigzag them together. Press the edges toward the dress and top stitch close to the ruffled edge.
3. Thread a needle and double the thread. Make a running stitch ³⁄₁₆" from the folded edge of the neck opening.

4. Place the dress on the chicken and pull the thread to gather the neck to fit her neck. Glue or stitch the button onto the front for a brooch and drape the lace around her arms for a shawl.

A NIGHTINGALE NAMED FLORENCE

Florence has a good heart: she has a sizable inherited income and is very generous toward her friends and relatives. She is frugal and conservative; she buys clothes from the local dry goods store and drives a no-frills American car. Florence does have a tendency to be very bossy, however; she berates her niece, "Get a perm in that hair of yours, for heaven's sake," and, to her sister, "Marge, you shouldn't be doing those dishes. Get your kids to do them!" She has been known to descend upon poor Marge's house and rip through it in a cleaning frenzy. Of course, while she is cleaning, so are her eight little nightingale nieces and nephews. No wonder they came to dread Aunt Florence's visits until, in desperation, they learned to spot her car and hide until she was gone.

Materials Requirements

◆ ⅓ yard of fabric for the body and the wings
◆ 10" x 12" piece of fabric for the legs
◆ Stuffing
◆ ⅓ yard of fabric for the dress
◆ 6½" square of lace or other suitable apron material
◆ ½ yard of ¼"-wide satin ribbon for apron ties
◆ Scrap of ¹⁄₁₆"-wide satin ribbon for bow
◆ ⅓ yard of ½"-wide lace
◆ Five ribbon roses for headband
◆ Delta fabric paint (see chart)

Assembly Instructions

Follow the directions for Jeannie on page 18, Steps 1-4. Substitute black Fabric Dye for yellow when you paint the beak.

Clothing

1. Follow the directions for Jeannie's dress, Steps 1-4. Instead of the ruffled ribbon, stitch the ½"-wide lace to the lower hem of the dress. Tie the narrow ribbon into a bow and glue it to the front neck of the dress, in place of the brooch.
2. Make a narrow hem on three sides of the apron (if necessary) and a ⅜" casing on top. Thread the ¼"-wide ribbon through the casing, gather the apron slightly, and tie a bow at the back of the dress.
3. Tack the ends of the ribbon rose leaves together to form a wreath. Place the wreath on the nightingale's head and glue it in place.

•

CHAPTER TWO

SMALL CLOTH ANIMALS

I am a member of the Betsy Buttons Cloth Doll Club. Each month, we meet to learn new techniques and show each other our latest projects. I asked this small but wonderful group to interpret some of the patterns in this chapter. Afton Nelson used the giraffe pattern to create Garafa Claus and wrote the following:

> Santa's so busy,
> I could help if I'd try.
> My neck could do chimneys
> and with practice I'd fly.
> Huge loads? Why, they'd be easy,
> Easy as pie.
> And people would get to Garafa Claus,
> By and by.

The rabbit, The Great Marco, is made from velvet. His creator Kay Stockseth edged his felt vest and trousers with narrow rickrack, used tiny buttons for eyes, and stitched tiny shoelaces from embroidery thread. Kay's daughter, Jean Marshall, made two giraffes. Herbert is conservative and traditional; Jasper is "up in the night," to use Jean's father's expression.

General Assembly Instructions

1. Pin the patterns to the fabric and cut them out. Make tailor tacks to designate areas that need to be marked, such as darts.
2. Transfer the face to the fabric by using a Sulky Iron-On Transfer Pen (see page 8, Step 1) or another method, such as tracing the face directly onto the fabric with a #2 lead pencil. When you use a transfer pen, remember you will be transferring a mirror image, so make the necessary adjustments.

3. Place the fabric with right sides together and stitch around the body, leaving an opening as indicated on the pattern piece. Trim the seam allowance and clip the curves. Turn the body right side out.
4. Stuff the body firmly, starting in the feet and working upward. Use small amounts of stuffing at a time and fluff each piece so the body won't be lumpy. If you want the animal to be able to sit, stuff the legs to within ½" of the top of the legs and top stitch across them. You may also use this method for the arms. (The teddy bear's ears are slightly stuffed, then top stitched across the top of the head.) Hand stitch the opening closed.

5. Follow the directions on each individual pattern for attaching separate ears, painting, embroidery, etc.

UNCLE WAYNE —
A DEBONAIR GIRAFFE

At 5' 6", I am rarely considered short except in my own family. I am the eldest and also the shortest. My brothers are all about 6' 5" and fairly thin. The most playful of these brothers is Wayne; he is adored by all the family, but most of all by his nieces and nephews. When he comes to our house, the kids all tackle him and want to ride on his back, wrestle with him in the backyard, and ride with him in his truck. Just for extra insurance, he usually has a bag full of treats for them. When I finished the giraffe, something about him reminded me of Wayne, so he was instantly christened.

Materials Requirements

◆ ½ yard of fabric for the body
◆ 2 black beads, ³⁄₁₆" wide
◆ Scrap of cloth for the horns
◆ 7" of 1½"-wide paisley satin ribbon for bow tie
◆ 13" of ⅝"-wide ethnic-looking braid or ribbon for suspenders
◆ Stuffing
◆ ⅙ yard of fabric for pants

Assembly Instructions

1. Tape the giraffe body pieces together, joining the head to the lower neck and body. Follow the General Assembly Instructions.
2. Place the ear pieces with right sides together and stitch around the ear, leaving an opening at the bottom (the straight edge). Trim the seam allowance and turn the ear right side out. Press it and turn the raw edges inside. Hand stitch the opening closed and pin the ear on the giraffe's head, toward the back seam. Note the pattern piece for placement. Stitch the ear to the head.
3. Place the giraffe's horns with right sides together. Stitch around each horn, trim the seam allowance, and turn the horn right side out. Stuff the horn very firmly and turn the raw edges inside. Since the horns are so small and may be difficult to stuff, I suggest you use a bamboo skewer. Stitch the opening closed and sew the horns to the giraffe's head as indicated on the pattern piece.

CLOTHING

TROUSERS

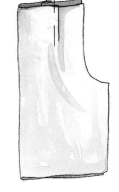

1. Pin the pleats so they overlap toward the front and back centers of the trousers. Baste them in place.
2. Place the trousers with right sides together and stitch the front and back seams. Clip the curves and press the seams open.
3. Cut a piece of fabric 1⅜" x 7" for the waistband. Fold one end of the waistband ½" and press it. Pin the folded end to the center front of the trousers (with the right side of the waistband on the wrong side of the trousers), overlapping the center seam ¼".

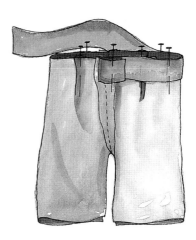

Stitch the waistband to the trousers. Trim the seam allowance and press it toward the band.
4. Press under ¼" of the waistband, fold the waistband over the raw edges of the waist toward the right side of the trousers, covering previous

stitching, and pin it in place. Top stitch the waistband.

5. With the right sides of the trousers together, stitch the inseam. Zigzag the lower edge of the trouser leg, fold up a ¼" hem, and machine stitch it in place. Press the trousers.

6. Cut two 6½" pieces of ⅝"-wide ethnic-looking braid (or other ribbon that looks like appropriate suspender material) and hand stitch the ends to the wrong side of the trousers back, crossing the suspenders at an angle.

You may wish to try the trousers on the giraffe to see exactly how the suspenders will best fit him. Mark the ribbon at the appropriate place and tack the suspender fronts to the inside of the trousers at the top of the pleats.

7. Make a bow tie by folding a 5½" length of 1½"-wide ribbon in half so the raw ends are centered in the back. Stitch them in place. The remaining 1½" of the ribbon may be folded around the bow to serve as a center. You will need to gather the ribbon slightly so the center won't be too wide. Hand stitch the center at the back of the bow tie. Find a scrap of ¼"-wide satin ribbon in a matching color and place it around the giraffe's neck. Stitch it together at the front and glue or stitch the bow tie at the center front.

HOWLING PAUL, THE COYOTE ON THE BALL

Every circle of friends has the ultimate party animal. The animal neighborhood seems to gather at Howling Paul's den each weekend. No one will ever forget the New Year's Eve party when Paul and his friends Ron and Bruce dressed up as the Supremes to lip sync their hit songs. Paul, the church choir accompanist, likes to confuse the choir members by playing the ending chord of a cappella numbers a half step higher than the actual notes, making the singers think they've gone flat (only, of course, in practice sessions). Paul's attractive spouse, Shirlene, complements his occasional lunacy by her quiet sense of humor.

Materials Requirements

- ⅓ yard of fabric for the body
- ⅙ yard of fabric for the vest
- ⅙ yard of fabric for the vest lining
- ¼ yard of trim, ribbon, or braid to decorate the vest
- Scrap of fabric for the bandanna
- Stuffing
- Black felt-tip fine-point permanent marking pen
- Powder blush
- Delta Fabric Dye Violet

Assembly Instructions

1. Follow the General Assembly Instructions, but use the felt-tip pen to trace the eyes onto the fabric. When the animal is stuffed, use a cotton swab to apply the blush to the cheeks (and the inside of his ears when they are finished).

2. Place the ears with right sides together and stitch around them, leaving an opening at the bottom. Trim the seam allowance, turn them right sides out, and tuck ¼" of the raw edges inside. Stitch the opening closed, press the ears, and stitch them to the coyote's head, noting the pattern for placement.

3. Place the tail with right sides together and stitch around it, leaving an opening for turning. Trim the seam allowance, clip the curves, and turn the tail right side out. Stuff it firmly and tuck ¼" of the raw edges inside. Stitch the opening closed and set the tail aside. It will be attached to the outside of the vest.

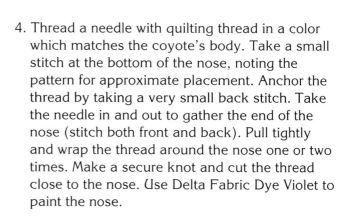

4. Thread a needle with quilting thread in a color which matches the coyote's body. Take a small stitch at the bottom of the nose, noting the pattern for approximate placement. Anchor the thread by taking a very small back stitch. Take the needle in and out to gather the end of the nose (stitch both front and back). Pull tightly and wrap the thread around the nose one or two times. Make a secure knot and cut the thread close to the nose. Use Delta Fabric Dye Violet to paint the nose.

CLOTHING

VEST

1. Fringe the lower edges of the front and back pieces of the vest and lining. The fringe should be ½" long.
2. Place the vest front and back with right sides together and stitch the shoulder seams. Repeat this step for the lining. Press all the seams open.
3. Place the vest and lining with right sides together and stitch the armholes and the neck edge.

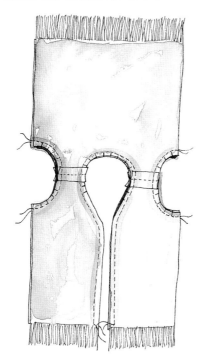

Clip the curves and turn the vest right side out.

4. Place the vest and lining with right sides together so the arm holes form a circle. Stitch the lining to the vest at the underarm seam and press it.

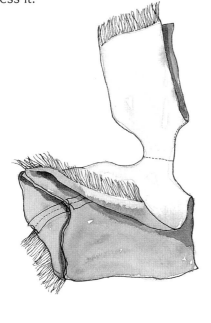

5. Fold under ¼" of the end of the ribbon or braid you have chosen to embellish the vest. Stitch it to the outside of the vest, just above the fringe. You may also use your sewing machine and rayon thread to add a decorative border around the neck edge of the vest.
6. Place the vest on the coyote and pin the tail to the outside of the vest at the back left side of the coyote's body. The tail will be on the same side of the body as the ears. Stitch the tail to the vest and to his body to secure it. Use quilting thread or other strong thread.
7. Cut a 5½" square of fabric for the bandanna. Use rayon thread in your machine to zigzag the edge of the bandanna instead of hemming it. The zigzag should not be wider than ⅛". Press the bandanna, fold it diagonally, and tie a square knot at the back of the coyote's neck.

MIKEY BEAR

When I told my children I was naming the giraffe after their uncle, Michael said he wanted me to name an animal after him. I asked him which one, and he said, "the little teddy bear." Somehow I thought that was fairly appropriate, so I present Mikey Bear to you. Mikey is the youngest and the darling of the family. Being rather independent, he enjoys the affection he gets, but wants people to know he has his own viewpoints, too. Mikey is wearing a sweater his mother bought for him. She liked it because she knew it would keep him warm when he went to school, but Mikey hardly ever wears it because he prefers T-shirts.

Materials Requirements

◆ ¼ yard of muslin for the body
◆ Stuffing
◆ Black embroidery floss
◆ Delta Fabric Dye Light Brown, White, Adobe, English Yew
◆ Delta Textile Medium
◆ #0000 brush
◆ #2 soft brush
◆ Scrap of cloth for the shorts
◆ Mismatched argyle sock for the sweater
◆ Scrap of ribbon for the bow tie

Assembly Instructions

1. Follow the General Assembly Instructions.
2. Embroider the eyes, nose, and mouth with a

single strand of black embroidery floss. Make a French knot for the eyes, wrapping the thread around the needle three times. (When I embroider after the animal is stuffed, I do not make a knot in the embroidery floss. Just bring the needle from the back of the head to the front, leaving a tail. Take a small anchoring stitch, catching two or three threads, and back stitch to outline the facial features. After you make the French knots, take the needle back out the back of the head next to the tail and make a small knot. This will be covered when you paint the bear.)

3. Mix equal quantities of the light brown paint and the textile medium. Use the larger brush to paint the entire body, except the inner eyes. When you get close to the embroidered features, use the small brush and be careful not to get paint on the floss.

4. After the paint is completely dry, add white paint to the eye. The iris will be painted green. Mix the white and adobe paints in equal proportions and paint the insides of the ears, the insides of the hands, the cheeks, and the bottoms of feet as indicated on the pattern.

CLOTHING

SHORTS

1. Place the shorts with right sides together. Stitch the front and back center seams. Clip the curves and press the seams open.

2. Zigzag the lower edges of the shorts. With right sides together, stitch the inseam.

3. Zigzag the upper edge of the shorts, fold under ¼" and machine stitch. Fold up ¼" of the lower edge of the shorts and machine stitch. Place the shorts on the bear.

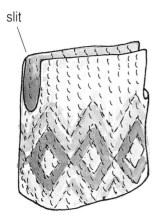

slit

ARGYLE SWEATER

1. Cut out the sweater pieces, following the sock diagram for dimensions and placement. Make a 1" slit down each side at the top of the sweater middle. Open the slits so they are in a straight line.

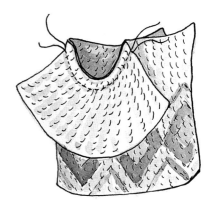

Place the sleeves and the sweater with right sides together and stitch them.

Turn the sweater wrong side out and zigzag the neck opening and bottom edge of the sweater. Stitch the shoulder seams from the neck to the arms, and turn the sweater right side out. Turn under a narrow hem at the neck and bottom edge of sweater if you wish. Place the sweater on the bear.

CHELSEA COW

Chelsea is a quiet, serious little cow. Her grandmother has shown her how to weave wreaths from wheat, so she is on her way home to make several more. Chelsea has just recently started to sew and she has her own sewing machine. It's very small and sews only a chain stitch, but Chelsea is very pleased with it.

Becky Tuttle designed this wonderful little cow and, when she showed it to me, I thought it might be just the right size to sit on a shelf. My thanks to Becky and All Cooped Up, Inc., for sharing this little cow from her *Barnyard Potpourri* pattern. (In addition to the cow, the *Barnyard Potpourri* pattern includes a pig, bear, cat, duck, and lamb.)

Materials Requirements

◆ ¼ yard of fabric for the dress
◆ ⅛ yard of fabric for the face and arms
◆ ⅛ yard of fabric for the apron
◆ 2" x 4" muslin scrap for the feed bag
◆ Small cow bell
◆ ⅓ yard of narrow twine
◆ Bits of dried flowers
◆ Delta Fabric Dye Adobe, Gold, Black
◆ Black felt-tip fine-point permanent marking pen
◆ Powder blush
◆ Poly Pellets
◆ Stuffing
◆ Potpourri

Assembly Instructions

1. Trace around the head pattern on the wrong side of the fabric. This is your sewing line. With right sides together, sew around this line, trim the seams, and clip the curves. Turn the head right side out and stuff it to within ¾" from the bottom opening. Gather the ears as indicated on the pattern. Paint the horns gold and the ears adobe. Paint black spots on the head using the photograph as a guide. Use the felt-tip pen to draw the eyes.

2. Trace around the muzzle on the wrong side of the fabric. On the right side of the fabric, trace the mouth with the marking pen. Place the right sides of the fabric together and stitch on the outline as you did for the head, but leave no opening for turning. Clip a small opening in one layer of the muzzle and turn through the opening. Press the muzzle and embroider the nose with a single strand of black embroidery floss. Make a French knot by wrapping around the needle three times. Glue or stitch the muzzle to the face.

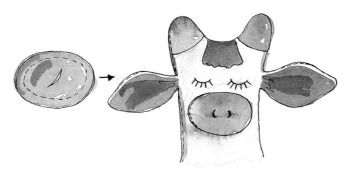

3. Hand gather the circle for the body ¼" from the edge, using quilting thread or four strands of regular thread. Pull up the gathers to make a pouch. Fill the bottom of the body with ¾ cup of the plastic pellets. This can be placed in a small plastic bag or poured directly into the body. Fill the rest of the pouch with stuffing mixed with potpourri. (You may substitute cotton balls soaked with essence oil.) Pull the gathers tight and tie them in a knot.

4. With right sides together, sew the arms, leaving them open where marked for turning. Trim the seam allowance and turn them right side out. Stuff the arms, leaving about 1¼" unstuffed in the center. Paint black spots on the ends of the hands.

5. With right sides together, sew the sleeves along the long edge. Turn them and slip the arms through the sleeve. Fold ¾" toward the inside, leaving ½" of the hands exposed. Gather the ends of the sleeves ¼" from the folded edge. Pull the gathers around the arm and tie a knot. Wind the quilting thread around the center of the arms and sleeves to gather them, then tie a knot.

6. Center the arms over the body, covering the gathered seam of the body. Tack or glue them in place.

7. Fold ½" of the bottom edge of the head to the inside. Pinch the sides of the head together so the seams meet. This should make the front and back form a point. Center the head over the arms, keeping the front and back slightly pointed, and glue or sew the head in place.

8. Tear a piece of fabric 10" x 1½" for the apron. Leave both edges torn. Gather the apron ¼" from one long edge. Pull up the gathers to 3". Center the apron over the body with the ends tucked under the arms. Tack or glue the apron in place.

9. Slip the twine through the cow bell and tie it in a bow around the base of the neck. Trim the ends of the bow.

10. With right sides together, sew around the feed bag. Turn it right side out and stuff it to within ¾" from the top. Slip pieces of dried flowers in the top of the bag and tie a piece of twine or raffia around to close it. Glue the feed bag to the cow's right arm.

NANNA COTTONTAIL

This sweet little rabbit is named after a little girl called Nanna by her family. Nanna is dressed up in a ballerina costume, consisting of gathered wire-edge ribbon and painted toe shoes. She loves dancing so much, she asked her mother if she could take dance lessons instead of going to pre-school. She also loves dressing up, having tea parties, and reading stories to her little brother. She enjoys baking molasses cookies and often hums her favorite songs while helping her mother in the kitchen.

Materials Requirements

◆ Scrap of muslin for the body
◆ Stuffing
◆ Black Sulky Iron-On Transfer Pen
◆ Black felt-tip fine-point permanent marking pen
◆ 2 yards of 1½"-wide wire-edge ribbon

- Delta Fabric Dye Light Mauve, Starlite Dye Lavender, LiquidHearts™ Opal, and Stencil Magic Paint Creme® Mauve
- Small satin rose
- ⅓ yard of ⅛"-wide satin ribbon
- ⅔ yard of narrow trim (beads, braid, or sequins)

Assembly Instructions

1. Follow the General Assembly Instructions. Stuff the ears lightly and top stitch them as indicated on the pattern piece.
2. Use a cotton swab to apply a small amount of Paint Creme to Nanná's cheeks, closed eyelid, and inside of ears. You will need a very small amount of paint and should try it out on a scrap of muslin first. Use the felt-tip pen to outline the eyes, whiskers, and mouth. Use the light mauve paint to fill in the nose.
3. Paint the leotard and shoes lavender. Use the opal paint for the tights, and let the paints dry thoroughly. Cut two 6" pieces of ⅛"-wide satin ribbon. Center the ribbon on the bunny's heel and use a needle and thread to tack it in place. Bring the ribbon to the front of the ankle and tie a small bow. Trim the ends of the ribbon and put a dot of glue in the center of the bow so it won't come untied. Glue narrow trim to the top of the bodice, starting in the back on the side, going over the arm, across the front, and over the other arm. Trim the legs of the leotard in the same manner and add a headband.
4. Gather the wire-edge ribbon by pulling out one of the wires to shirr the ribbon. Glue the gathered ribbon around her waist, circling it three times, with the raw ends in the back. Use your fingers to arrange the gathered ribbon to look like a tutu. Embellish the waistline with a ribbon rose and the ⅛"-wide satin ribbon tied into a bow.

•

PAPER CLAY ANIMALS

My children and their friends had a wonderful time playing with Paper Clay, but so did some of my adult friends. Among the creations I received were two circus animals designed by Kim Brown from Salt Lake City. She sent Popo the Elephant and Mary Lou the Russian Bear. They arrived at my house through the underground animal railroad. I think they have decided to settle down in one of the charming cottages and stay for a while. They have already met some of their neighbors and especially enjoyed Paul's get-acquainted party.

Betts Vidal reduced the small mouse body pattern on the photocopy machine to make a charming set of three pigs. Rather than using fabric for their feet and hands, she made them from Sculpey. True to the story, the pigs carry straw, sticks, and bricks to build their new homes. As good neighbors should, they have come to help their new friends build a strong brick wall.

Shauna Mooney Kawasaki has also created a wonderful Paper Clay animal. This magnificent Egyptian bird is larger than most of the other animals. Shauna used the same basic body as I used for the elephant; she designed her own feet and hands, which she sewed on to make the bird larger.

Ellie Elephant and Polly Pig are my daughter Vanessa's creations. Ellie is dressed in a length of

eyelet lace for a skirt, pearl-edged ribbon around her waist, and a small satin bow in front. Narrow lace is glued around her neck, with a satin ribbon rose at the throat. Ellie is dressed in the same style Vanessa chooses for herself. Polly Pig is ready to go to school. She has a narrow ribbon bow at the top of her head, a wider ribbon at her throat, and gathered wire-edge ribbon for her skirt. She is 5½" high.

After Michael's first attempt at creating an animal (which turned out to be a snowman), I encouraged him to try again. He made the mouse and painted it by himself. The body is pink fabric and the bow tie is a 1½"-wide ribbon, just like Uncle Wayne's.

Clinton made several animals, but one of my favorites is his coyote. This very sophisticated character was inspired by a Markus Pierson poster we bought in a Santa Fe gallery. Clinton enjoyed playing with the clay more than any of the rest of the children; he seemed to have more patience in shaping the head and refining it. I helped him create the glasses by shaping floral wire and cutting out small circles of black construction paper. I glazed the paper with a thick layer of clear Delta Cool Stuff and also used it to glue the paper to the wire.

Bruce seemed to enjoy the Paper Clay as much as Clinton. His hound and pheasant heads have wonderful personality and detail. The hound's body is filled with Poly Pellets and his only decoration is his bow tie. The pheasant's body and wings are made from hand-dyed fabric which I machine quilted with rayon thread. Arthur, the pig I created, also employs the wonderful hand-dyed fabrics from Skydyes (by Mickey Lawler, 83 Richmond Lane, West Hartford, CT 06117, telephone 203-232-1429).

PAPER CLAY

Paper Clay is a remarkable product made from paper pulp, volcanic ash, water, and a few other ingredients. It doesn't have to be cured in an oven; let it air dry for a day or two. Once hardened, the project can be sanded and painted. Here are a few tips for a successful experience with Paper Clay:

1. Knead the Paper Clay until it is smooth before you begin to form your creation. Use sculpting tools (which are available at art supply stores) if you wish, but you can probably devise your own tools from items around your home.
2. To keep the clay from drying, dip your fingers in a cup of water from time to time to keep the surface of the project moist, but not dripping. If you have to leave the project for a few minutes, be sure to wrap it with plastic while you are gone.
3. When you need to apply a separate part to the body, such as an ear or nose, moisten the body area and rub it a little until it feels slightly sticky. Attach the part to the sticky surface and push it inward without damaging the overall shape. It is a good idea to do this before you work on fine details.
4. To create flat surfaces, such as the pig's ears, use a doll-size rolling pin or a large dowel to roll the clay flat. Old scissors may be used to cut out the shapes. When you make the eyes, use a dull pencil or a similar object to make an eye socket. Make a small, round ball for the eyeball, moisten it, and push it into the socket. You may also use a bead for an eyeball. Push the bead into the socket to make sure it fits, remove it, and glue it in place after the animal is dry and painted.
5. To conserve Paper Clay, roll up a ball of aluminum foil and mold the clay around the foil ball. (This is a good way to recycle used aluminum foil.)
6. When sculpting an animal, divide the head into geometrical shapes; for example, the pig snout and neck are shaped like cylinders, the head is a sphere, the cheeks are hemispheres, and the

ears are triangles. The mouse face is a cone and the back of the head is rounded.

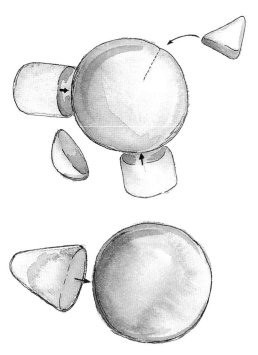

7. Be sure to create a flat surface so the head can stand up while it is drying. Make an indentation around the lower part of the neck so you can wire the body securely.

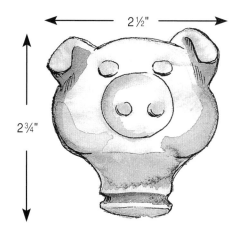

2½"
2¾"

8. If you are in a hurry to finish your Paper Clay project, dry it in the oven for 10 to 20 minutes at 200°. Otherwise, let it sit undisturbed for 24 to 48 hours before you sand it. Make sure the inside of the piece has dried thoroughly as well. If any of the body parts fall off, you can use a small amount of tacky glue to re-attach them.
9. When the head is completely dry, sand the surface first with a metal fingernail file. I have even used small nail scissors to trim away excess clay. Nylon tulle may be used for fine sanding. Tie loose knots, close to each other, and use the knots to sand the clay project.

10. Use a good quality acrylic paint, such as Delta Ceramcoat, to finish the animal head. If you like a shiny finish, use an acrylic varnish after the paint has dried. Above all, have fun with Paper Clay. Re-live the wonderful hours you spent in grade school making snakes and cookies from oil-base clay. Don't worry whether your animal looks perfect: a few flaws give character to your creation.

SCULPTING TOOLS FOR PLAYING WITH CLAY

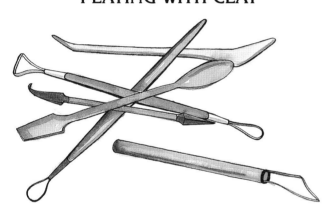

Basic Materials Requirements

- ½ package of Paper Clay for each animal head
- Delta Ceramcoat acrylic paints
- Sculpting tools (see above)
- Assorted fabrics (¼ yard or less for the bodies and scraps for the clothing)
- Fusible web
- Bits of lace, ribbon, and trims
- Floral wire
- Pipe cleaners

General Assembly Directions

See page 28 for specific information on how to work with Paper Clay. You may also use some of the general sculpting techniques to create heads from other mediums, such as Sculpey or Cernit.

1. Cut out the body pattern and zigzag the neck opening. Place the right sides of the fabric together and stitch around the body. Trim the seam allowance and clip the curves. While the body is still wrong side out, fold down ¼" of the neck opening to form a casing. Since it will be difficult to machine stitch, you will probably need to use a small running stitch next to the zigzagged edge in order to stitch the casing.

2. Stuff the body firmly, starting with the legs. When you get to within ½" of the top of the leg, if you want the animal to be able to sit, top stitch across the top of the leg. Stuff the arms and repeat the same technique if you want the arms to bend. If your animal has wings, place a little bit of stuffing in the ends of the wings and use your machine to top stitch the wings. Note the pattern for stitching lines. Continue stuffing to the top of the neck. Clip the threads in one of the side seams, just inside the casing.

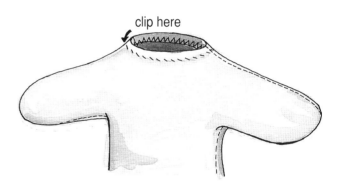
clip here

3. Cut a 6" piece of floral wire, bend ¼" of one of the ends so it won't catch in the fabric, and insert the wire into the casing through the seam you just clipped. Feed it carefully all the way around the casing and out the same hole. Insert the head and pull the wires to gather the casing around the neck. Twist the wires, clip them about ¼" from the neck, and bend them around so they stick back down between the neck and the casing.

4. If the animal needs (or requests) a tail, cut a rectangle 6¼" x 1¼". Fold the tail in half with right sides together and stitch one end, and along the sides of the rectangle. Trim the seam allowance. Turn the tail right side out by using a small safety pin or a turning tube. Insert a pipe cleaner and clip it about ¼" shorter than the tail. Fold the raw edges inside and stitch the tail to the animal, noting the pattern for placement. Dress the animals using some of the following general clothing instructions.

BASIC CLOTHING ASSEMBLY INSTRUCTIONS

THE FIELD MICE

Although I was never happy to see a mouse scurrying across the floor in our house, I enjoyed seeing them outside. Occasionally, my father would discover a nest in the barn or other outbuildings, and we would all run to see the tiny newborn mice smaller than our fingers. When I made these two mice, I decided to make sisters. I was fortunate enough to have three sisters, but Sonia was just a year younger than I, and we are especially close friends. We enjoy many of the same activities and always enjoy dressing up for special occasions. These mouse sisters are dressed for an evening at the ballet.

Materials Requirements

- ⅙ yard of fabric for both bodies
- Stuffing
- Scraps of lace for a collar
- Small ribbon roses
- Skirt fabric (4" x 30" for the larger mouse and 3¼" x 28" for the smaller)
- 20" piece of 1½"-wide ribbon for each mouse's sash
- Lace to trim the bottom edge of the skirt (28" of ⅝"-wide lace was used on the smaller mouse's skirt)

Clothing Assembly Instructions

1. Glue the lace around the neck and attach a small ribbon rose at the center front.

2. If you want to trim the skirt with lace, place the lace and the raw edge of the fabric with right sides together. Zigzag them together and press toward the skirt. If you are using lace for the skirt, there is no need to line it.
3. Gather the top edge of the skirt to fit the mouse's waist. Fold the skirt in half so the back edges are together. Stitch the back seam and press it open. Pull the skirt over the mouse's feet, pin it to the waist area, and tack it to the body with a needle and thread.
4. Tie the ribbon around the mouse's waist and tie a bow in the back of the waist. Trim the ribbon to an inverted V. The tails should be no longer than 2¼". The bow will be approximately 2" wide.

HENNY PENNY

I don't think Ben intended this chicken to become Henny Penny, but that's what I instantly thought of when I saw it. When my family and I were visiting in Ketcham, Idaho, this summer, we stopped in a wonderful gift shop. I found the tiny vegetables and knew they were just the right size for Henny Penny to carry from market. You can make your own vegetables from Paper Clay. Henny is in a hurry to get back home, since she wants to avoid running into Foxey Loxey.

Materials Requirements

- ¼ yard of fabric for the body
- Stuffing

- Scrap of fabric for the apron
- 7" of ⅜"-wide satin ribbon for the neck
- Scrap of lace for the neck
- 21½" of ¼"-wide satin ribbon
- White acrylic fabric paint

Clothing Assembly Instructions

1. Zigzag around the entire apron. Zigzag around the pocket top.
2. Press under ¼" of the pocket sides. Top stitch across the top of the pocket. Top stitch again ¹⁄₁₆" below the first stitching. Stencil the pocket with the tiny heart design. After the paint is dry, pin the pocket to the apron, noting the pattern for placement. Stitch the sides and bottom of the pocket to the apron.

3. Press under ¼" around all edges of the apron. Baste a 5½" length of ¼"-wide ribbon to the top of the apron.

   Cut two 8" lengths of ribbon and baste them to the sides. Stitch around the entire apron, ¹⁄₁₆" from the edge, then top stitch again ¹⁄₁₆" from the first stitching.
4. Place the apron over the chicken's head, glue a lace collar around her neck, tie a 1" bow, and trim the ends in an inverted V. Glue the bow to the front of the neck.
5. Find a small basket and fill it with small vegetables. Hang the basket over the hen's wings and tack the wings together so she can hold the basket.

FELIX

Clinton decided to call his cat Felix. The only Felix I remember from my childhood, aside from the cartoon, was a hired hand whose ability to spit tobacco juice was quite incredible. I doubt whether he ever wore a tuxedo in his life, but somehow the incongruity appealed to me.

Materials Requirements

- ¼ yard of fabric for the body
- Stuffing
- Paper-backed fusible web
- Scraps of white fabric
- Scraps of ⅜"-wide satin lavender ribbon
- Scraps of ⅛"-wide satin purple ribbon
- Tiny beads or rhinestones

Clothing Assembly Instructions

1. Cut two 6" squares of white fabric. Cut a piece of paper-backed fusible web and fuse the wrong sides of the fabric together, following the manufacturer's directions. Pin the tuxedo shirt and collar patterns to the fused fabric and cut them out. If you want to use a product to stop the fraying you may, but it is not necessary. Top stitch the tuxedo as indicated on the pattern piece.

2. Glue or stitch small beads or rhinestones down the center of the shirt front. Place the collar around the cat's neck and glue it in back. Place the narrow purple ribbon around the center of the collar and glue it in front.

   Make a small bow tie (⅞"-wide) by folding a piece of ⅜" satin lavender ribbon with the ends in the middle. Fold a piece of ⅛" satin ribbon around the center and glue it in the back. Glue the bow tie to the front of the collar.

TURTLE

1. Place the feet and tail with right sides together and stitch them. Trim the seam allowance, turn them right side out, and stuff them softly. Place them on the turtle body, with the raw edges together, and baste them in place.
2. Place the turtle body with right sides together and stitch it, leaving an opening at the top. Finish the casing as instructed on page 29, Step 1. Fill the body ½ full of pellets and lightly stuff the rest of the body to the neck. Insert the head, pull the wire taut, and twist it.
3. Make a bow tie like Uncle Wayne's (page 22) and glue it to the front of the neck to finish your turtle.

PHEASANT

Materials Requirements will be the same as for Jeannie, page 17, eliminating the button for the brooch, the dress, and the ribbon roses for the hair. In addition, you will need:

◆ Fairfield Cotton Classic Batting
◆ Rayon thread for machine quilting
◆ ¼ yard of fabric for outer wings and tail
◆ ¼ yard of lining for outer wings and tail
◆ Yarn
◆ Paper Clay
◆ Delta Ceramcoat paints for the head

Bruce's pheasant instructions are similar to those of Jeannie and Florence, pages 17 and 19. Rather than creating an all-cloth body, you will be following the basic directions for Paper Clay animals on page 28 (Step 1) and the directions for Jeannie on page 18 (Steps 1, 2, and 4). Then continue with the following steps:

1. Cut out the wings and tail and place them on the batting with the right side of the fabric facing you. Loosen the top tension of the machine and lengthen the stitch to machine quilt the fabric to the batting.
2. Place the quilted fabric and the lining with right sides together and stitch around them, leaving an opening for turning. Clip the curves and turn the wings and tail right side out and press them. Stitch the wings to the body, curving them around the shoulder area toward the front of the body. There will be about an inch between the wings in the back. Pleat the tail, using the pattern as a guide. Tack the pleats in place. The tail will be stitched to the back of the body about 1½" above the crotch area.
3. Wrap yarn around cardboard several times. Thread a string through the middle of the wrap, at the top of one of the sides of the cardboard, then slip the yarn off the cardboard. Tie the string around the knee joint of the bird's leg and around the neck, if you want to. Glue it in place and clip the bottom ends of the yarn to create a fringe.

PROJECTS

(Back row): Florence (Miriam Gourley), Mephisto (MG), Uncle Wayne (MG), (front row): Mary Lou (Kim Brown), Christine (MG), Arthur (MG), Chelsea (Becky Tuttle); love seat and cottages (Bruce Gourley)

Popo (Kim Brown), Egyptian Bird (Shauna Mooney Kawasaki), Mary Lou (Kim Brown)

Kitty Blue (Barbara Johnston), Dotty and Spot (Barbara Johnston), Morgan (Bonnie Hoover); love seat (BG)

Turtle (Kyle Jensen), Dinosaur (Brent Staley), Arthur (MG); love seat (BG)

Mephisto (MG); hat boxes (MG)

Polly (Tracy Stilwell), "What Bird?" (Patti Culia), Cathouse Sunday (Karen Wooton)

L. Thorwald Frogg (MG); chair and ottoman (BG)

Nanna (MG), Mikey (MG), Chelsea (Becky Tuttle); cottage (BG)

Ellie (Vanessa Gourley), Dog (Jill Jensen), Polly (Vanessa Gourley), Henny Penny (Ben Jensen); cottage (BG)

(Back): Pheasant (BG); (front): Cool Coyote (Clinton Gourley), Mouse (Michael Gourley), Fox (Mindy Jensen), Hound (BG)

The Great Marco (Kay Stockseth), Herbert and Jasper (Jean Marshall), Garafa Claus (Afton Nelson); chair (BG)

Florence (MG), Butch (Thomas Gourley), Felix (Clinton Gourley); chair and bed (BG)

Three Pigs (Betts Vidal), Field Mice (MG); cottages (BG)

Copper Lady Cat (MG), Stan (MG), Blue Boy (MG), Christine (MG); chairs, ottoman, table, and cottage (BG)

Howling Paul (MG), Jeannie (MG), Uncle Wayne (MG); cottage (BG)

•

HOMES AND FURNISHINGS

As you leaf through decorating magazines, you will notice that most rooms have focal points—a fireplace, a picture window, or a painting. Sometimes the focal points are enhanced by vignettes, such as a fireplace mantle displaying a collection of antique dishes or toys. In my own dining room, I have an antique china closet filled with pink depression glass, my childhood tea set, and our wedding china. On the top of the closet, I put a favorite Anne of Green Gables character doll. Anne is standing near a white wicker chair surrounded by ivy which spills over the sides of the cabinet. Many of my friends say this makes it the coziest room in the house.

Since I think the cloth animals are meant to be displayed and would add a wonderful focus to any room, I wanted to include items which would enhance them and make a charming vignette. I decided to try to create furniture and houses that could have been made by the animals themselves. I asked my husband, Bruce, to help me make some willow furniture. One afternoon we gathered all sorts of nature's goodies from his parents' spare lot, and he retired to the basement to experiment. All sorts of graceful, artistic pieces of furniture and charming cottages began to take form: Bruce has found a new hobby. Be careful, or you might find this hobby as addicting as he has!

WAXED LINEN THREAD

We discovered this wonderful thread in a shop which specializes in products for caning chairs. The thread is 100% linen coated with wax. The wax makes it almost impossible for a knot to come loose, an invaluable asset when you are using it to construct the furniture. The thread comes in a wide variety of colors, but we selected the olive green because it is more congruent with the natural furniture materials. You can obtain the thread from The Caning Shop, 926 Gilman Street, Berkeley, CA 94710 (telephone 510-527-5010).

THE FURNITURE

1. Work with dry willow for the best results. Green willow will shrink as it dries, and the areas you join together will probably become wobbly. If you need to curve the willow, remember to use willows which are small in diameter. You may soak the willows overnight, or use green willow (cautiously) so it will bend more easily.

2. Use a drop of hot glue to tack the parts together, then bind them with waxed linen thread. Start by wrapping the thread diagonally around willow pieces a and b and tie a knot. Leave a tail so you can tie another knot at the end of this procedure.

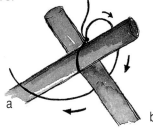

Wrap this same area twice, bring the thread halfway up and around to the left, then wrap it around willow a.

Wrap the thread diagonally in the opposite direction from Step 1. Repeat this twice.

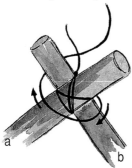

Bring the thread around between willows a and b to tighten the thread. Tie a square knot and clip the ends short.

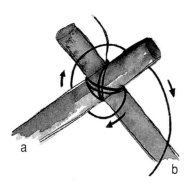

3. When you place willows close together to cover the surface of a chair or table, use a darning needle and the waxed linen thread to secure the willows to the frame. Leave a small gap so the needle can go between the willows. Tie the tail of your needle and thread to the frame where you wish to start. Bring the thread up over the first willow, back down under the base, then down and around the side frame of the chair and back to the third willow. Repeat the process, going to the fifth willow, then the seventh, and so on. Repeat this procedure until you come to the end of the willows on the surface of the piece. As you come to the end, repeat the sequence backward, bringing the needle and thread over the willows you missed the first time. Tie the thread where you began.

The charts show the basic items of furniture and their measurements.

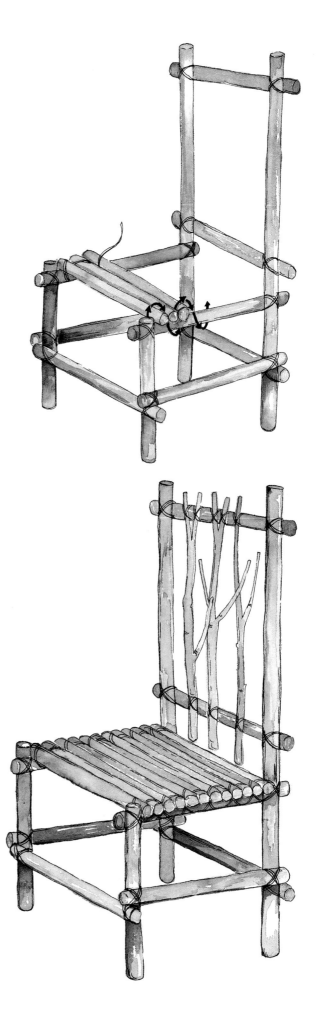

Chair: cut the following willows:

Quantity	Length	Part of Chair
2	4⅛"	Front legs
2	13½"	Back legs
4	5"	Bottom braces
1	5"	Lower back brace
1	5"	Top back brace
5	9½"	Long back rests
2	5"	Top seat side braces
16 to 20	4⅝"	Seat cover
2	About 12 to 12½"	Arm rests
1	About 7½"	Top arch (optional)

Ottoman: cut the following willows:

Quantity	Length	Part of Table
4	4⅛"	Legs
4	5"	Bottom leg braces
2	5"	Top side braces
16 to 20	4⅝"	Ottoman cover

Table: cut the following willows:

Quantity	Length	Part of Table
4	6⅝"	Legs
2	7"	Bottom side braces
1	7½"	Center bottom brace
2	7"	Top end braces
2	8"	Top side braces
20 to 25	8¼"	Table top

TABLE

BED

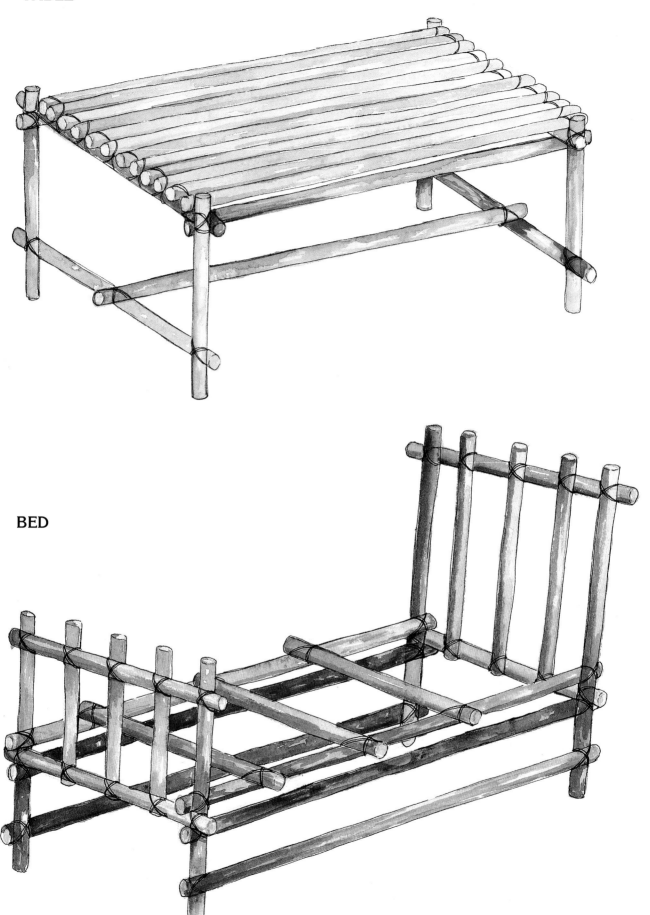

Bed: cut the following willows:

Quantity	Length	Part of Bed
2	4½"	Footboard legs
2	7½"	Headboard legs
1	6½"	Bottom footboard leg brace
1	6½"	Top footboard leg brace
3 to 5	2⅝"	Footboard vertical twigs
1	6½"	Bottom headboard leg brace
1	6½"	Top footboard leg brace
3 to 5	5¼"	Headboard vertical twigs
1	10"	Headboard arch twig (optional)
1	10"	Footboard arch twig (optional)
2	9¾"	Side braces
2	9¼"	Lower side braces
7	6¼"	Horizontal mattress slats

Love seat: cut the following willows:

Quantity	Length	Part of Love seat
2	4⅛"	Front legs
2	8"	Back legs
2	5"	Bottom side leg braces
1	10½"	Bottom back leg brace
1	10½"	Bottom front leg brace
2	5¼"	Side seat leg brace
1	10½"	Lower back leg brace
1	10½"	Top back leg brace
18 to 20	10½"	Seat cover
About 6	4¼"	Back rest twigs
About 4	3¼"	Side arm rest twigs (optional)
2	About 9"	Arched arm rests
1	About 18"	Back arch

LOVE SEAT

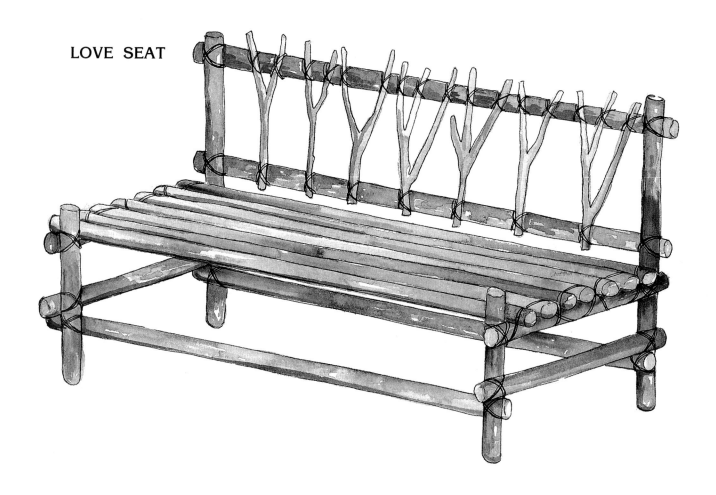

EMBELLISHMENT

Use a thin willow to create the curved arms for the love seat; the length will vary. Soak it overnight and bend it into a semicircle. Dry the willow with a paper towel and tack it to the back and front leg areas of the chair, then fasten it securely with the waxed thread. Repeat this procedure for the other side and back of the chair.

Many items can be used to decorate the furniture once the basic shape is constructed. Dried moss, dried flowers, sea shells, pods, pine cones, wood roses, dried berries, and many other objects found in your backyard or at a florist shop may be used. If you use dried berries, put a drop of tacky glue at the base of each berry to secure it to the branch. (When the berries continue to dry, they become loose and may fall off.)

BEDDING

1. To create a mattress, cut two pieces of fabric 7½" x 10¼". Place them with right sides together and stitch around all four sides, leaving a 3" opening.

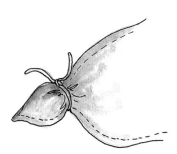

2. Make Turkish corners by wrapping thread around each corner about ¼" from the stitching.

Turn the mattress right side out and stuff it loosely.

3. To make a quilt, cut two pieces of fabric and a piece of Fairfield Cotton Classic Batting 11" x 11". Place the top of the quilt on the cotton batting, with the right side of the fabric on top. With the batting directly on the feed dogs, machine quilt the fabric in 1" vertical channels. Repeat for the horizontal channels.

4. Place the quilted fabric and the quilt lining with right sides together. Stitch around the quilt, leaving a 3" opening along one side. Turn the quilt right side out and stitch the opening closed. Top stitch ¼" from the outside edges.

5. Place the quilt on the mattress and tack the bottom corners so they don't flare out from the bed.

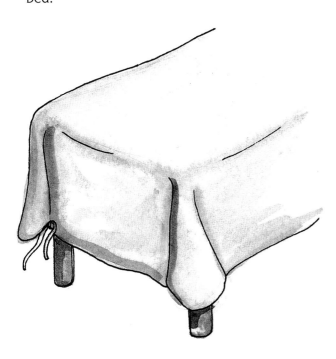

6. To make pillows, cut four 3¾" x 3¼" squares of fabric. Place the right sides together and stitch around all four sides, leaving a 2" opening. Turn the pillows right side out and stuff them. Stitch the openings closed.

THE COTTAGES

Materials Requirements

◆ Cylindrical boxes, such as from oatmeal or bread stuffing
◆ Delta Texture Ceramcoat or other textured acrylic paint
◆ Posterboard to make conical roofs
◆ Dried moss, pine cones, or commercial doll-house roofing shingles
◆ Willows
◆ Doll-house bricks
◆ Fabric
◆ Fusible web
◆ Dried flowers
◆ Small polished stones

General Assembly Instructions

1. Use the patterns for doors and windows and trace them onto the boxes. Cut the doors and windows out and lay them aside.
2. Use textured paint to cover the outside of the box. You may have to let the first layer dry and paint it a second time to cover any pictures on the box.

3. Cut a conical roof from the posterboard by using one of the following sizes of circle. You will need to use a pencil to divide the circle into quarters. Cut one or more of the quarters out and overlap the roof. Use a hot glue gun to bond it instantly.

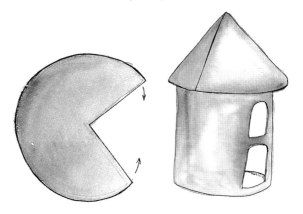

4. Use the glue gun to bond the roof to the house. Cover the outside of the roof with white glue and press dried moss or other roofing materials in place. You may also use a hot glue specifically recommended for wood if you choose miniature wood shingles (available from dollhouse suppliers).
5. Cut the window in half to form shutters. Cover them with small willows trimmed to the size of the shutter and glue them in place. Cover the door in the same manner and glue it to the outside of the house.
6. You may glue the house to some kind of a base, such as a board purchased at the craft store, and add dried flowers or moss around the house. It can also stand alone.
7. Bruce made a brick wall by covering a 1" x 3" piece of lumber (5" long) with miniature bricks from a doll-house supplier.

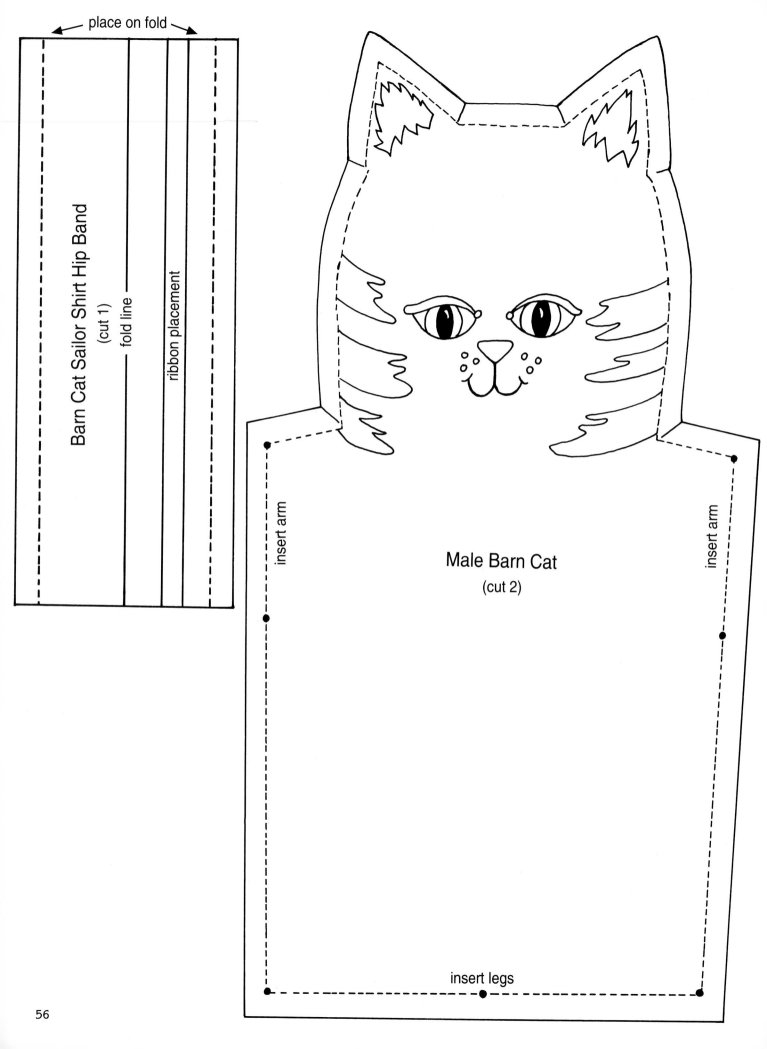

place on fold

Barn Cat Sailor Shirt Hip Band

(cut 1)

fold line

ribbon placement

insert arm

insert arm

Male Barn Cat

(cut 2)

insert legs

56

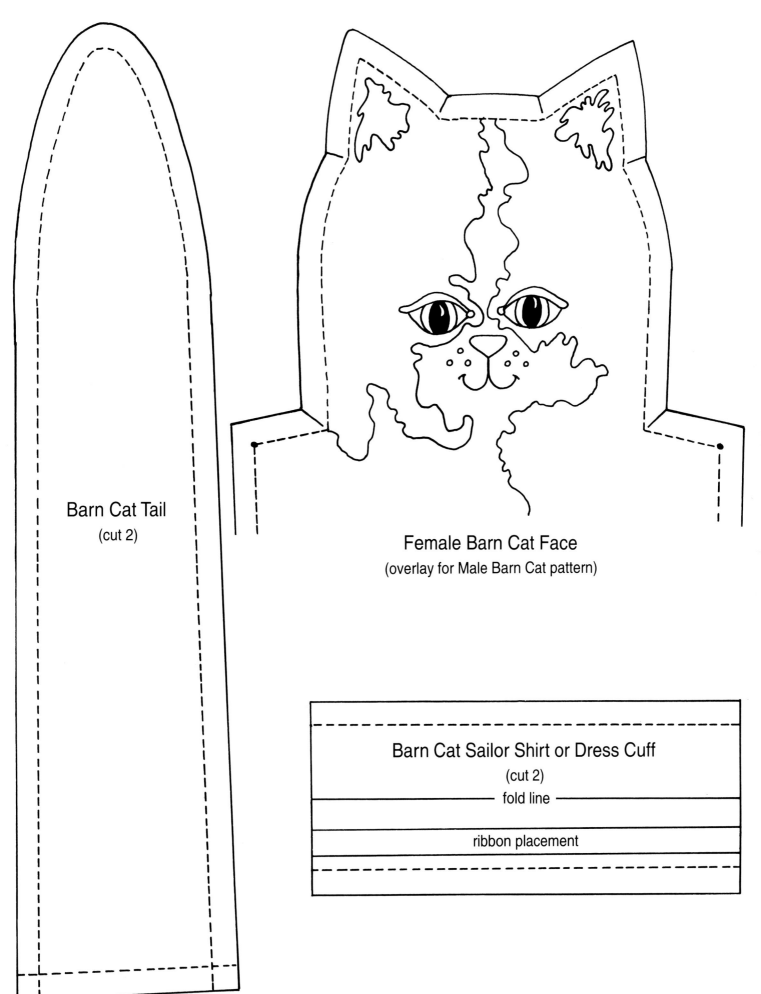

Barn Cat Tail
(cut 2)

Female Barn Cat Face
(overlay for Male Barn Cat pattern)

Barn Cat Sailor Shirt or Dress Cuff
(cut 2)
— fold line —

ribbon placement

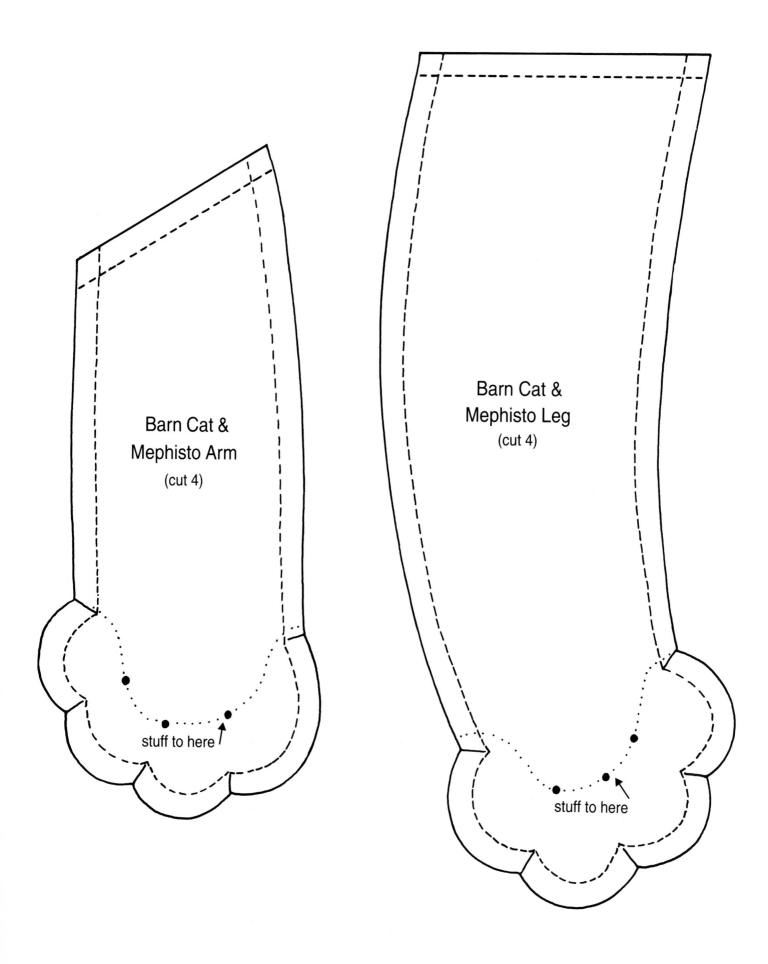

Barn Cat &
Mephisto Arm
(cut 4)

stuff to here

Barn Cat &
Mephisto Leg
(cut 4)

stuff to here

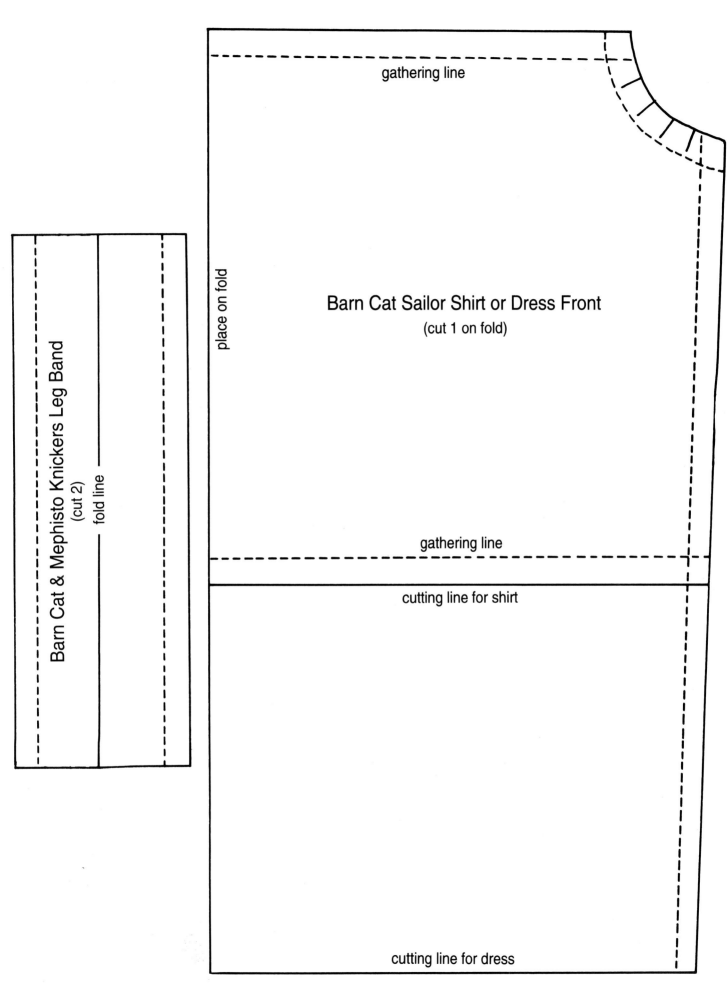

gathering line

place on fold

Barn Cat Sailor Shirt or Dress Front

(cut 1 on fold)

gathering line

cutting line for shirt

Barn Cat & Mephisto Knickers Leg Band

(cut 2)

fold line

cutting line for dress

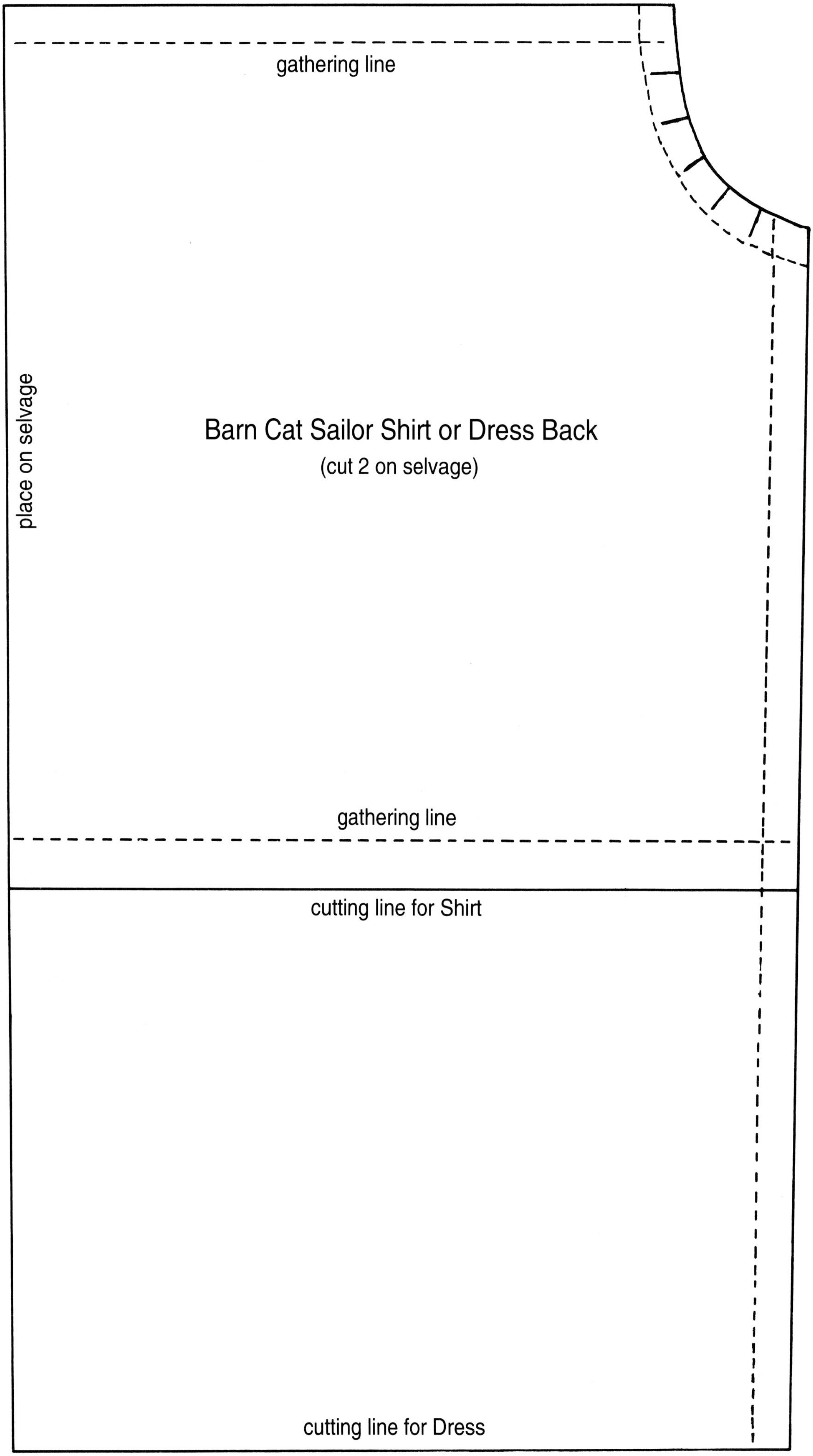

gathering line

place on selvage

Barn Cat Sailor Shirt or Dress Back

(cut 2 on selvage)

gathering line

cutting line for Shirt

cutting line for Dress

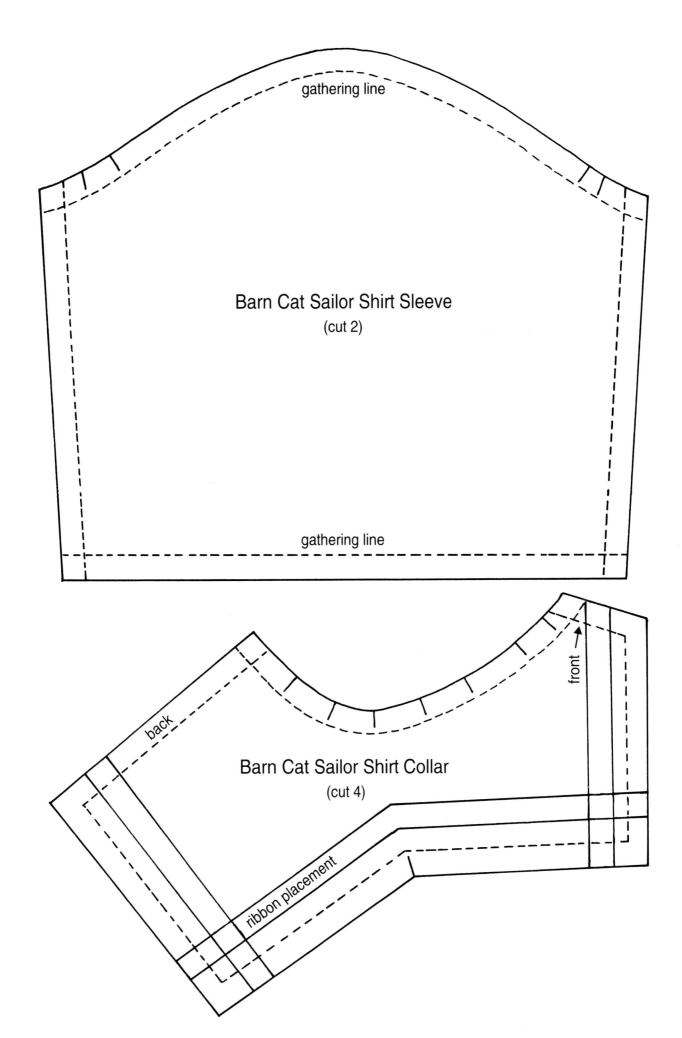

gathering line

Barn Cat Sailor Shirt Sleeve

(cut 2)

gathering line

back

front

Barn Cat Sailor Shirt Collar

(cut 4)

ribbon placement

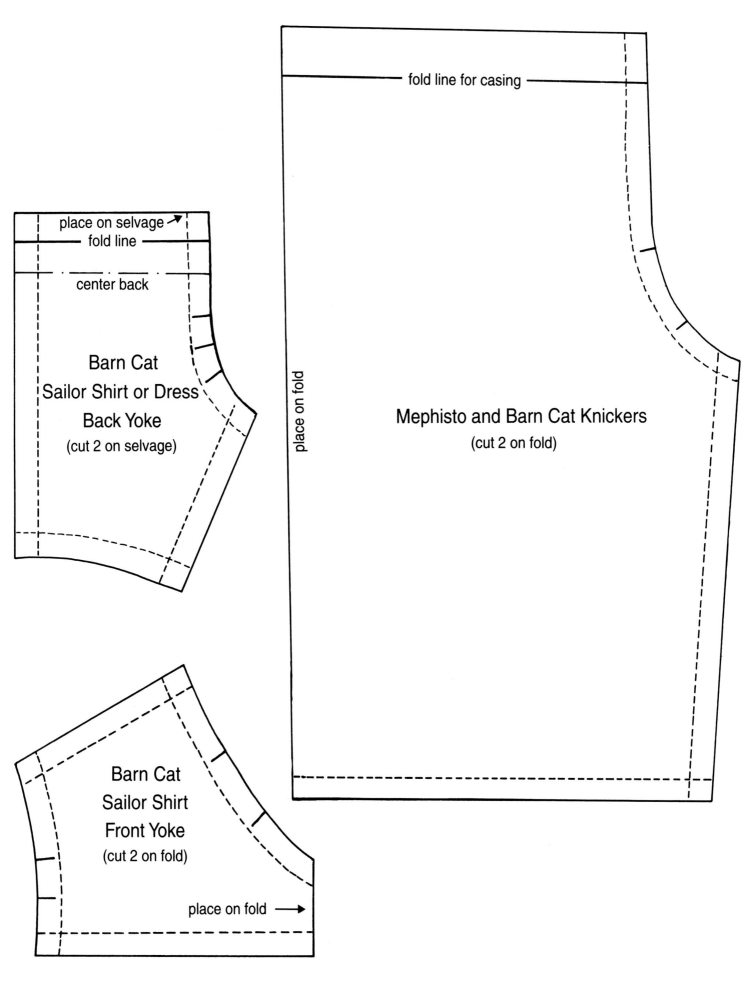

place on selvage
fold line
center back

Barn Cat
Sailor Shirt or Dress
Back Yoke
(cut 2 on selvage)

fold line for casing

place on fold

Mephisto and Barn Cat Knickers
(cut 2 on fold)

Barn Cat
Sailor Shirt
Front Yoke
(cut 2 on fold)

place on fold →

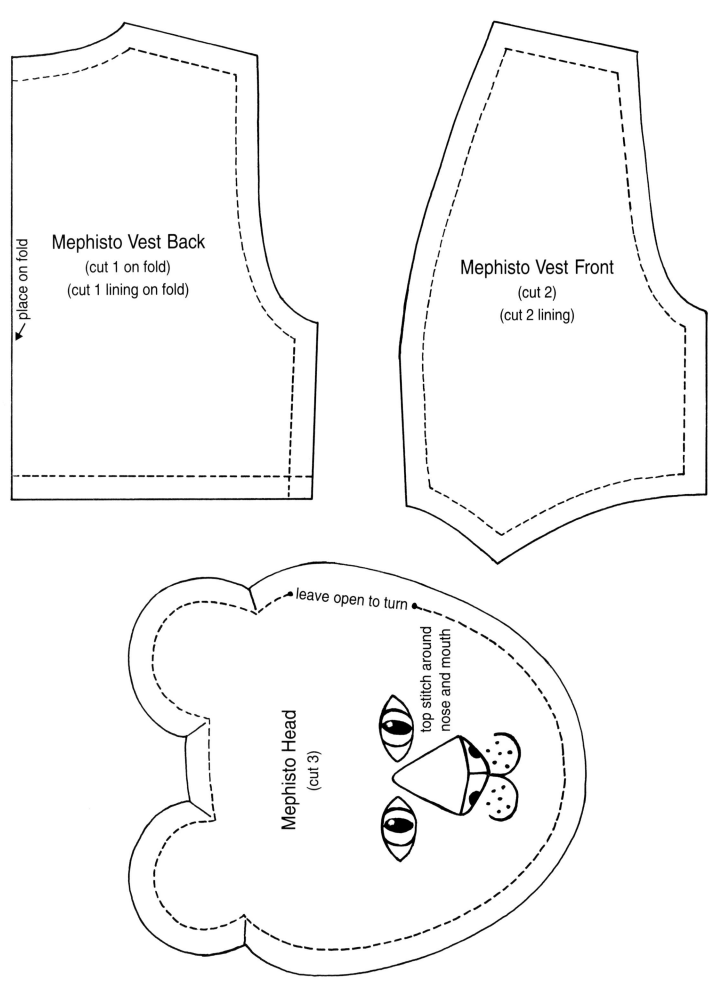

Mephisto Vest Back
(cut 1 on fold)
(cut 1 lining on fold)

place on fold

Mephisto Vest Front
(cut 2)
(cut 2 lining)

leave open to turn

Mephisto Head
(cut 3)

top stitch around nose and mouth

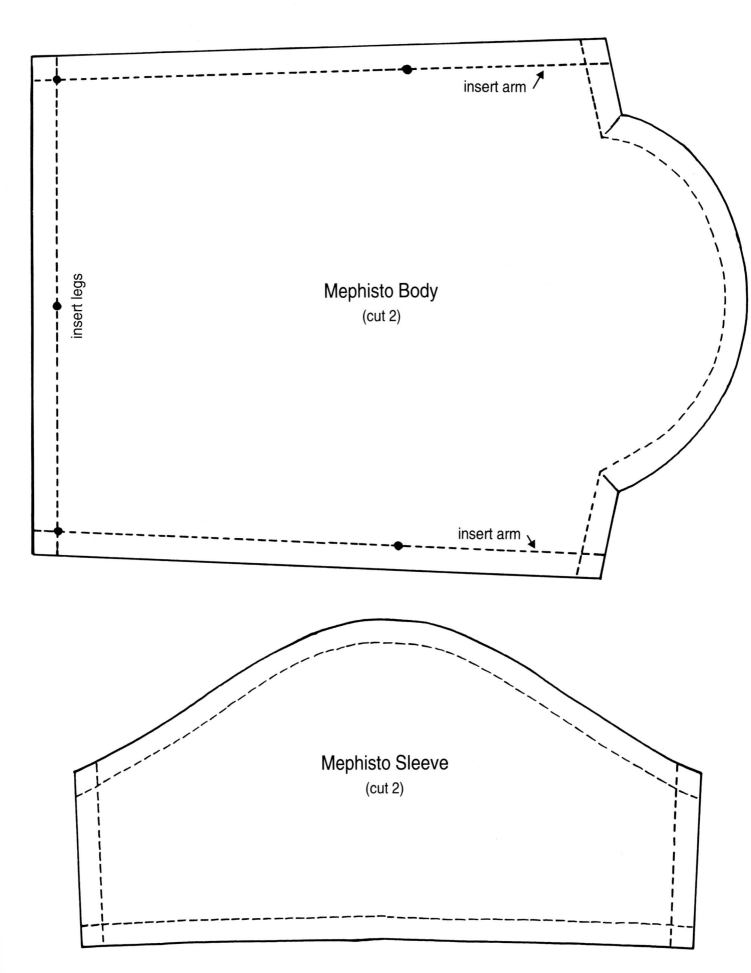

insert arm

insert legs

Mephisto Body
(cut 2)

insert arm

Mephisto Sleeve
(cut 2)

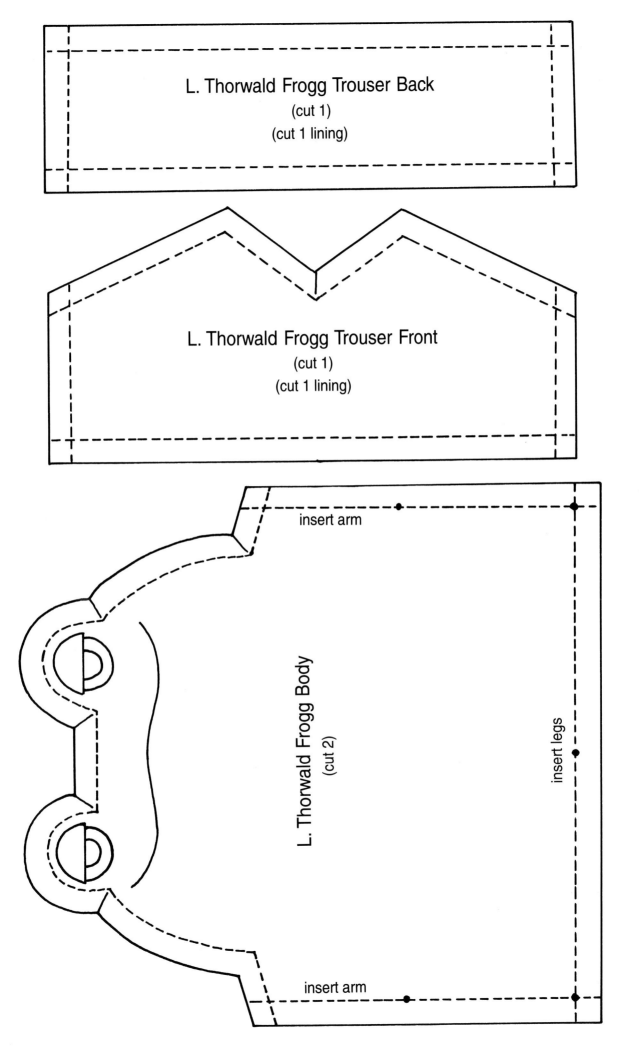

L. Thorwald Frogg Trouser Back
(cut 1)
(cut 1 lining)

L. Thorwald Frogg Trouser Front
(cut 1)
(cut 1 lining)

insert arm

L. Thorwald Frogg Body
(cut 2)

insert legs

insert arm

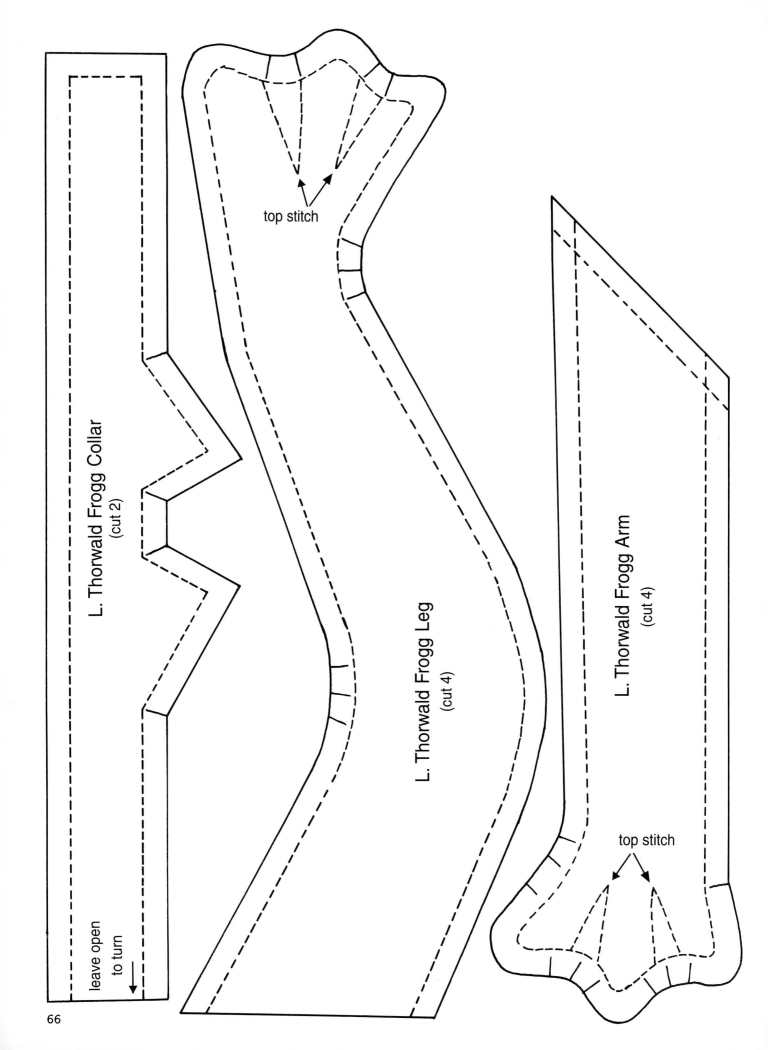

L. Thorwald Frogg Collar
(cut 2)

leave open
to turn

top stitch

L. Thorwald Frogg Leg
(cut 4)

L. Thorwald Frogg Arm
(cut 4)

top stitch

66

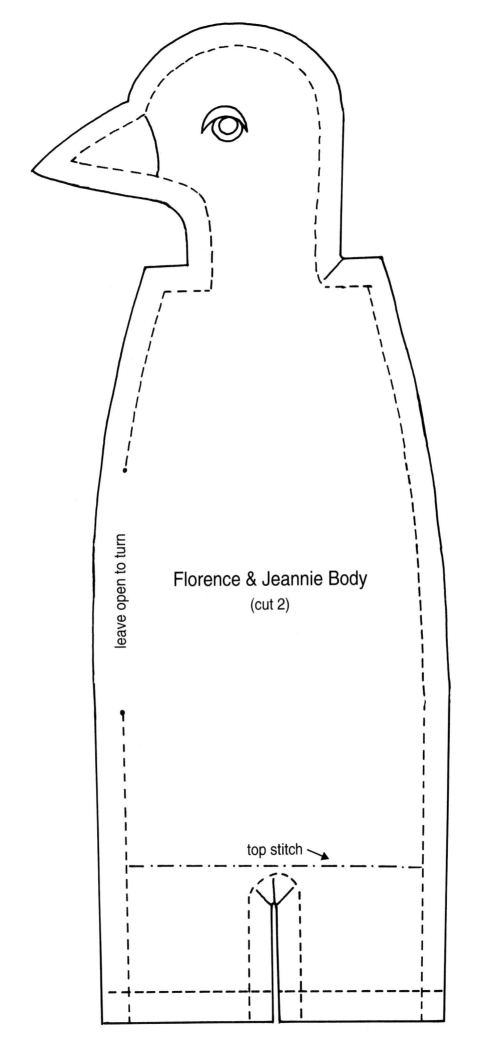

leave open to turn

Florence & Jeannie Body

(cut 2)

top stitch

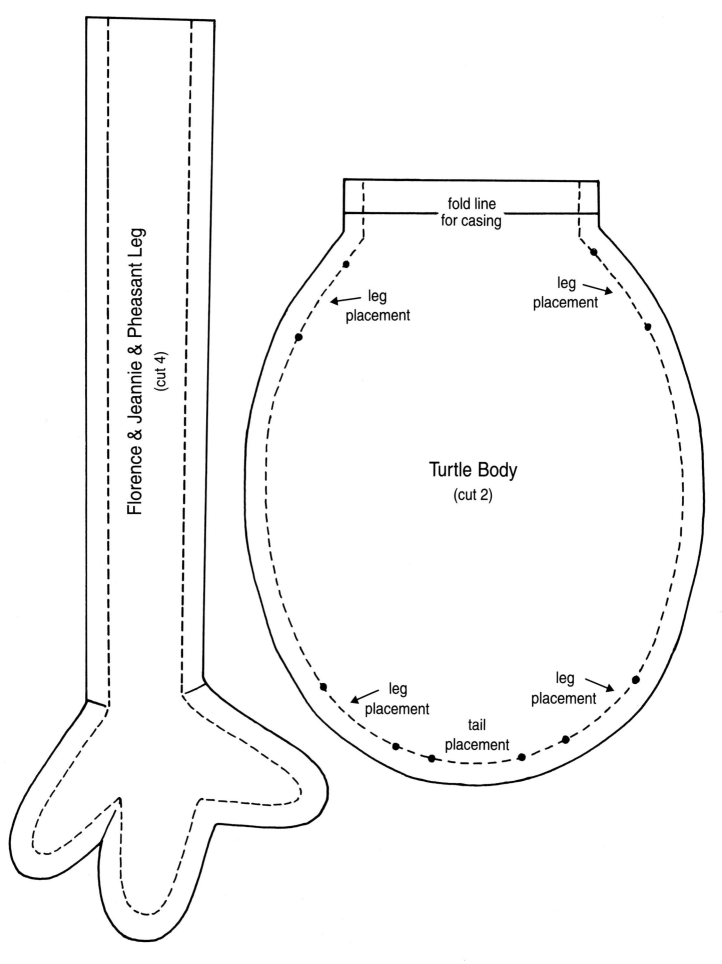

Florence & Jeannie & Pheasant Leg
(cut 4)

fold line
for casing

leg
placement

leg
placement

Turtle Body
(cut 2)

leg
placement

leg
placement

tail
placement

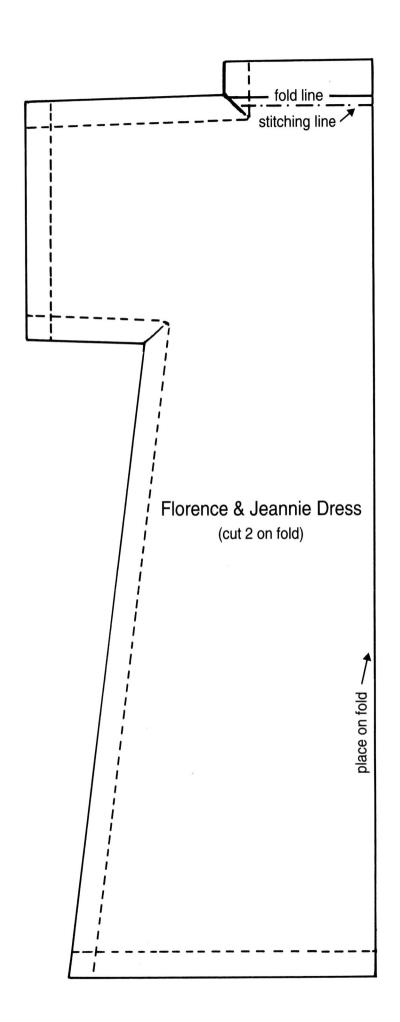

fold line

stitching line

Florence & Jeannie Dress

(cut 2 on fold)

place on fold

first arm

second arm

2 ¼"

slit to here

top of Sweater

slit to here

Mikey Bear Sweater

2 ½"

bottom of Sweater

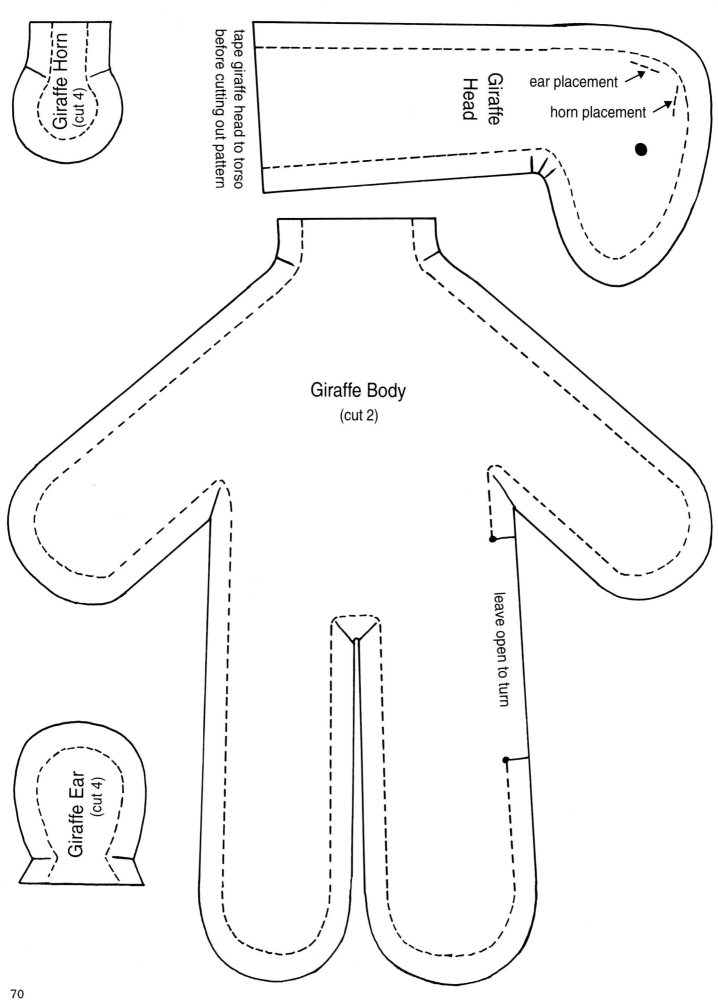

Giraffe Horn
(cut 4)

tape giraffe head to torso
before cutting out pattern

Giraffe
Head

ear placement

horn placement

Giraffe Body

(cut 2)

leave open to turn

Giraffe Ear
(cut 4)

70

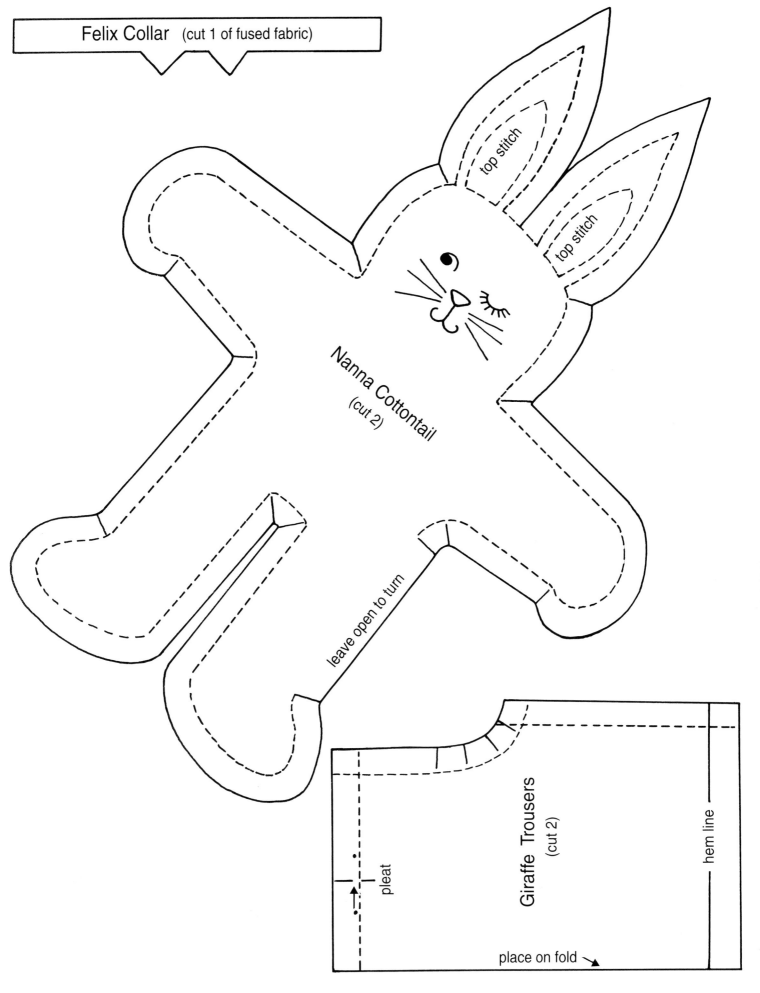

Felix Collar (cut 1 of fused fabric)

top stitch

top stitch

Nanna Cottontail
(cut 2)

leave open to turn

Giraffe Trousers
(cut 2)

pleat

hem line

place on fold →

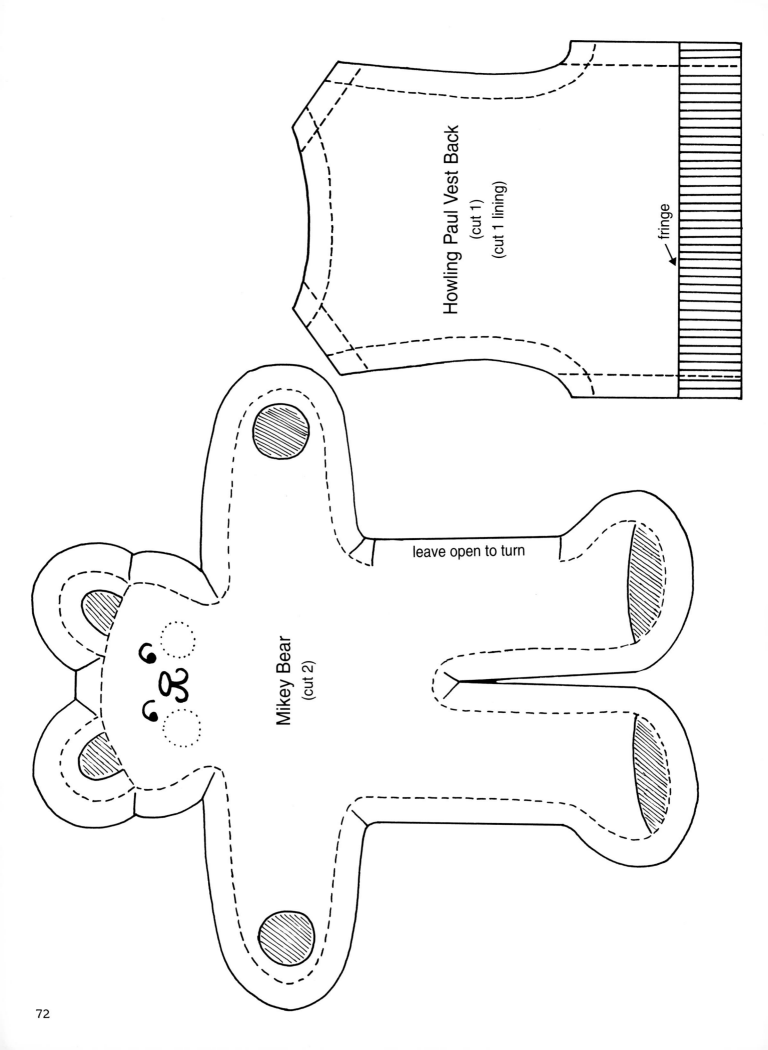

Howling Paul Vest Back
(cut 1)
(cut 1 lining)

fringe

Mikey Bear
(cut 2)

leave open to turn

72

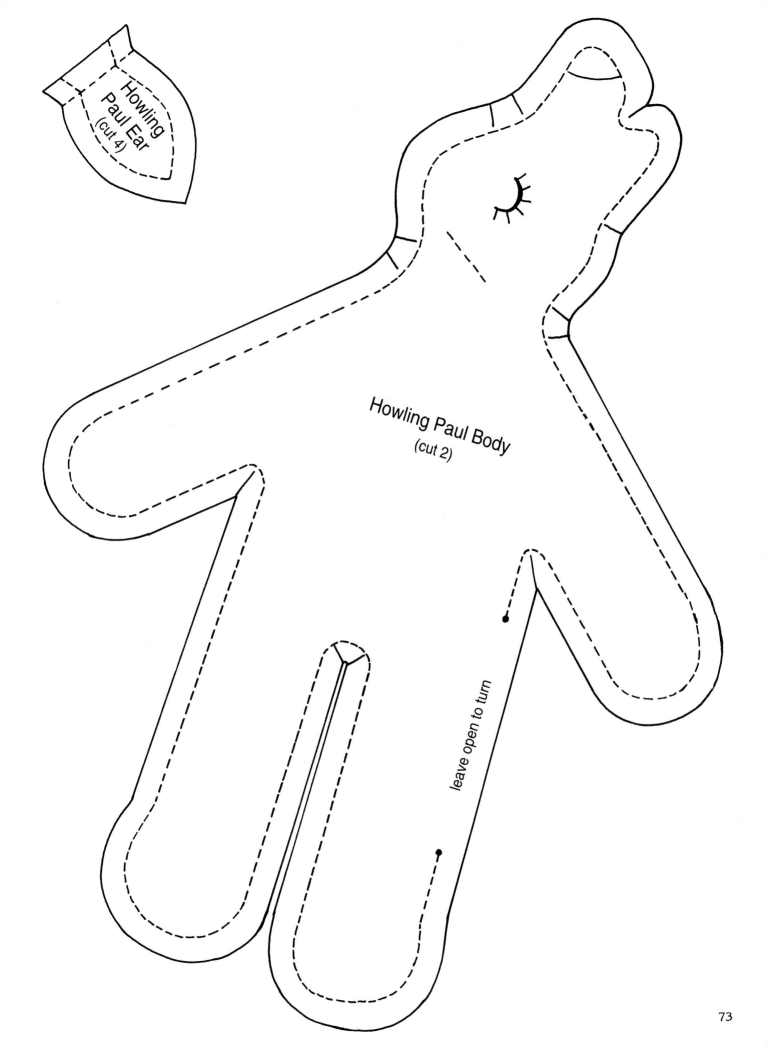

Howling
Paul Ear
(cut 4)

Howling Paul Body
(cut 2)

leave open to turn

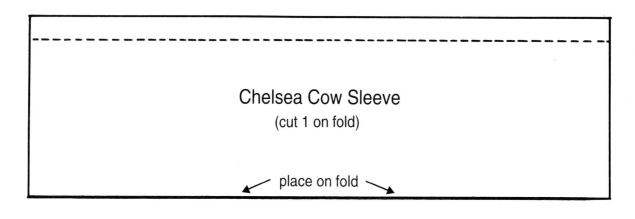

Chelsea Cow Sleeve

(cut 1 on fold)

←— place on fold —→

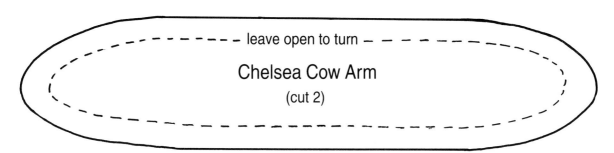

— — leave open to turn — — —

Chelsea Cow Arm

(cut 2)

Cow Muzzle

(cut 2)
(place 2 layers of
fabric together
and trace outline)

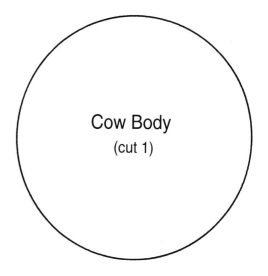

Cow Body

(cut 1)

Draw approximate 8" circle

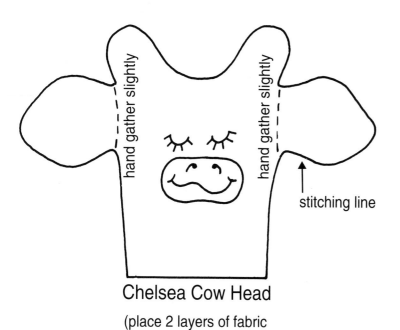

hand gather slightly

hand gather slightly

← stitching line

Chelsea Cow Head

(place 2 layers of fabric
together and trace outline)

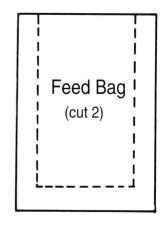

Feed Bag

(cut 2)

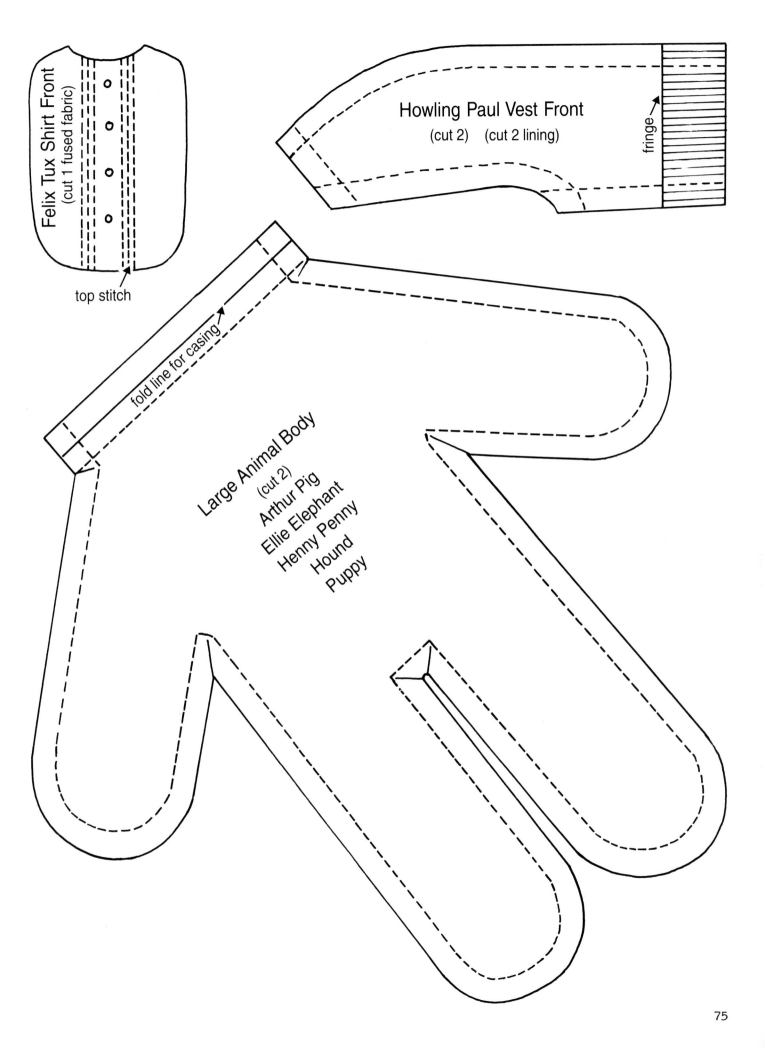

Felix Tux Shirt Front
(cut 1 fused fabric)

top stitch

Howling Paul Vest Front
(cut 2)   (cut 2 lining)

fringe

fold line for casing

Large Animal Body
(cut 2)
Arthur Pig
Ellie Elephant
Henny Penny
Hound
Puppy

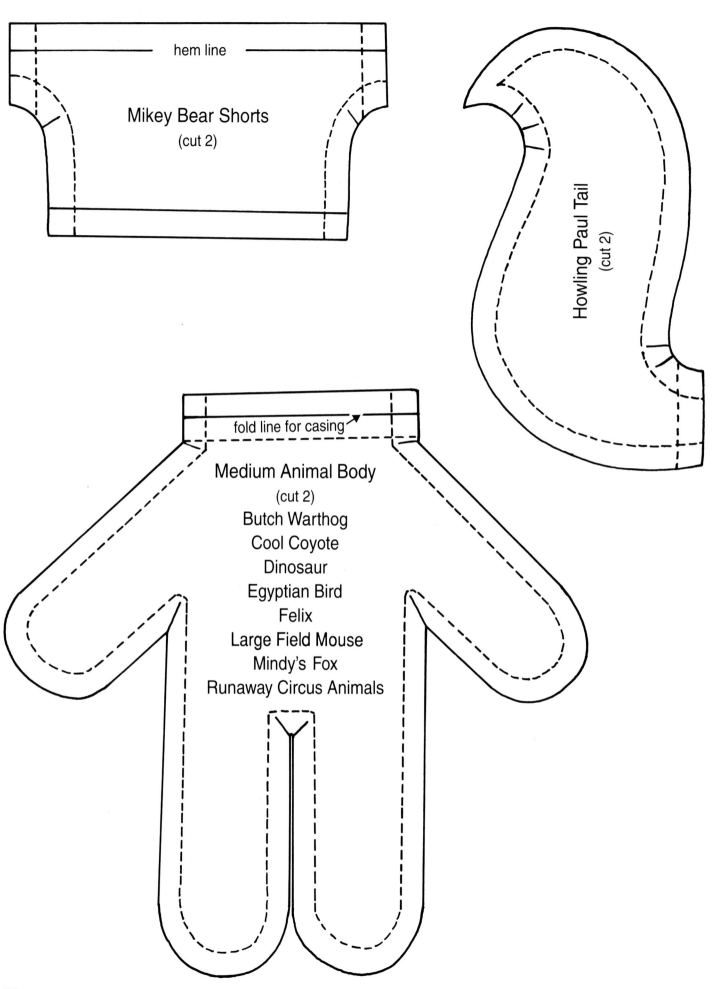

hem line

Mikey Bear Shorts
(cut 2)

Howling Paul Tail
(cut 2)

fold line for casing

Medium Animal Body
(cut 2)
Butch Warthog
Cool Coyote
Dinosaur
Egyptian Bird
Felix
Large Field Mouse
Mindy's Fox
Runaway Circus Animals

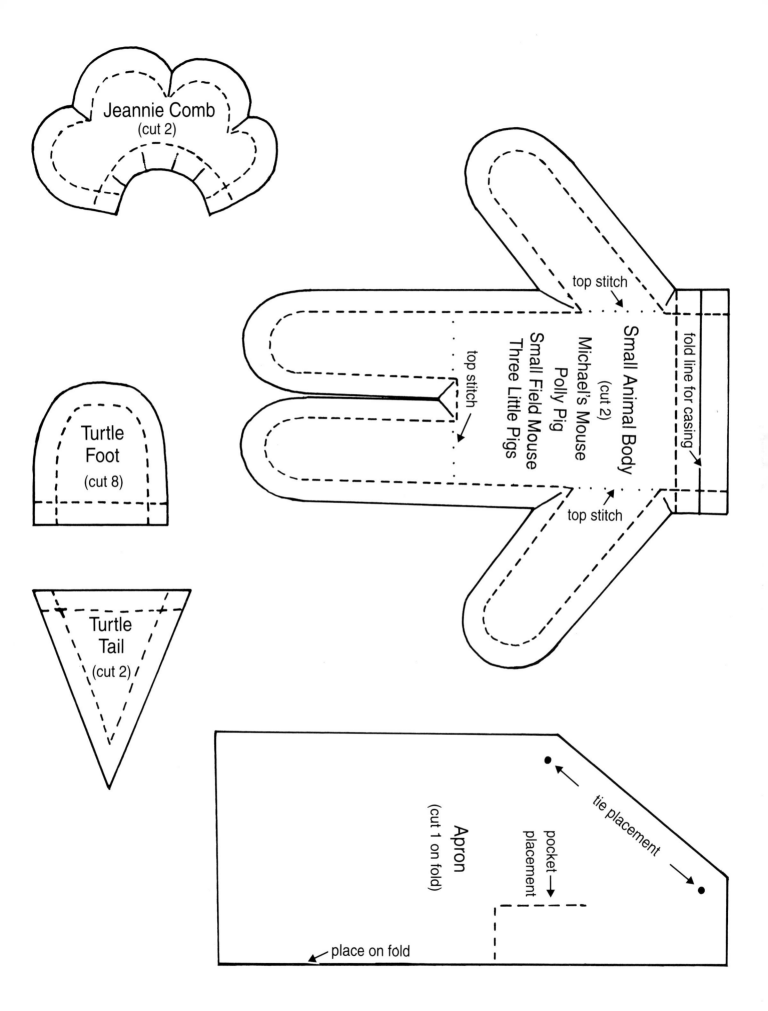

Jeannie Comb
(cut 2)

Turtle
Foot
(cut 8)

Turtle
Tail
(cut 2)

Small Animal Body
(cut 2)
Michael's Mouse
Polly Pig
Small Field Mouse
Three Little Pigs

top stitch

top stitch

top stitch

fold line for casing

Apron
(cut 1 on fold)

tie placement

pocket
placement

place on fold

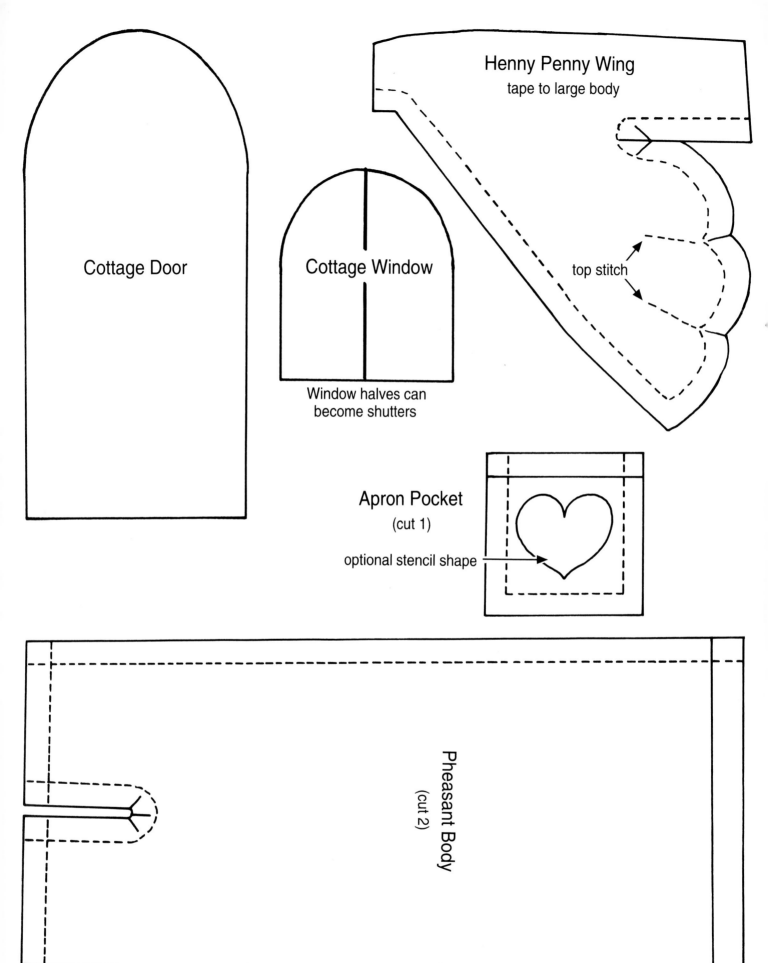

Cottage Door

Cottage Window

Window halves can
become shutters

Henny Penny Wing

tape to large body

top stitch

Apron Pocket

(cut 1)

optional stencil shape

Pheasant Body

(cut 2)

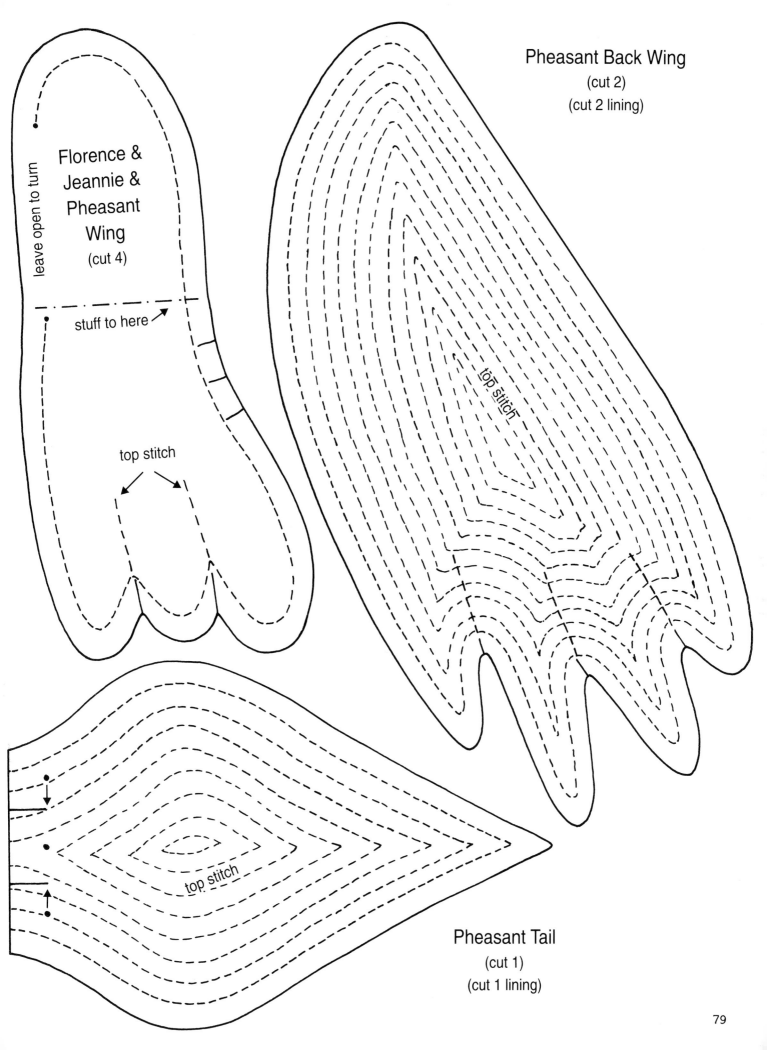

Pheasant Back Wing
(cut 2)
(cut 2 lining)

leave open to turn

Florence &
Jeannie &
Pheasant
Wing
(cut 4)

stuff to here

top stitch

top stitch

top stitch

Pheasant Tail
(cut 1)
(cut 1 lining)

Other Fine Quilting Books
From C&T Publishing

An Amish Adventure, Roberta Horton

Appliqué 12 Easy Ways!, Elly Sienkiewicz

The Art of Silk Ribbon Embroidery,
Judith Montano

*Baltimore Album Quilts, Historic Notes and
Antique Patterns*, Elly Sienkiewicz

Baltimore Beauties and Beyond (2 Volumes),
Elly Sienkiewicz

Boston Commons Quilt, Blanche Young and
Helen Young Frost

Calico and Beyond, Roberta Horton

A Celebration of Hearts, Jean Wells and
Marina Anderson

Christmas Traditions From the Heart,
Margaret Peters

Crazy Quilt Handbook, Judith Montano

Crazy Quilt Odyssey, Judith Montano

Design a Baltimore Album Quilt!,
Elly Sienkiewicz

*Dimensional Appliqué—Baskets, Blooms &
Borders*, Elly Sienkiewicz

Fans, Jean Wells

Fine Feathers, Marianne Fons

Flying Geese Quilt, Blanche Young and
Helen Young Frost

Friendship's Offering, Susan McKelvey

Happy Trails, Pepper Cory

Heirloom Machine Quilting, Harriet Hargrave

Imagery on Fabric, Jean Ray Laury

Irish Chain Quilt, Blanche Young and
Helen Young Frost

Isometric Perspective, Katie Pasquini-Masopust

Landscapes & Illusions, Joen Wolfrom

Let's Make Waves, Marianne Fons and Liz Porter

Light and Shadows, Susan McKelvey

Magical Effects of Color, Joen Wolfrom

Mariner's Compass, Judy Mathieson

Mastering Machine Appliqué, Harriet Hargrave

Memorabilia Quilting, Jean Wells

New Lone Star Handbook, Blanche Young and
Helen Young Frost

NSA Series: Bloomin' Creation, Jean Wells

NSA Series: Holiday Magic, Jean Wells

NSA Series: Hometown, Jean Wells

NSA Series: Hearts, Fans, Folk Art, Jean Wells

Perfect Pineapples, Jane Hall and Dixie Haywood

Picture This, Jean Wells and Marina Anderson

Plaids and Stripes, Roberta Horton

PQME Series: Milky Way Quilt, Jean Wells

PQME Series: Nine-Patch Quilt, Jean Wells

PQME Series: Pinwheel Quilt, Jean Wells

PQME Series: Stars & Hearts Quilt, Jean Wells

Quilting Designs from Antique Quilts,
Pepper Cory

Recollections, Judith Montano

Story Quilts, Mary Mashuta

Treasury of Quilt Labels, Susan McKelvey

Trip Around the World Quilts, Blanche Young and
Helen Young Frost

Visions: Quilts of a New Decade, Quilt San Diego

Working in Miniature, Becky Schaefer

Wearable Art for Real People, Mary Mashuta

3 Dimensional Design, Katie Pasquini

For more information write for a free catalog from:

C & T Publishing
P.O. Box 1456
Lafayette, CA 94549
(1-800-284-1114)